Critical Guides to German Texts

EDITED BY MARTIN SWALES

DÜRRENMATT

Der Besuch der alten Dame *and* Die Physiker

Kenneth S. Whitton

Professor Emeritus
Department of European Studies
University of Bradford

Grant & Cutler Ltd
1994

© Grant & Cutler Ltd 1994

ISBN 0 7293 0362 4

I.S.B.N. 84-599-3367-9

DEPÓSITO LEGAL: V. 267-1994

Printed in Spain by
Artes Gráficas Soler, S.A., Valencia
for
GRANT & CUTLER LTD
55-57 GREAT MARLBOROUGH STREET, LONDON, W1V 2AY

For S.J.F.B.

Contents

Preface

Friedrich Dürrenmatt's works were published in definitive versions, authorized by the writer, by the Diogenes Verlag AG, Zürich, in 1980. This *Werkausgabe*, in the detebe paperback series and edited by Thomas Bodmer, is in twenty-nine volumes, with a thirtieth, a volume of critical writings, *Über Friedrich Dürrenmatt*, and contains what Dürrenmatt called the 'literarisch gültigen' versions of his works.

These differ, in some cases substantially, from other versions; the editions of *Der Besuch der alten Dame* and *Die Physiker*, published in Great Britain by Methuen (now Routledge) and Macmillan (now Nelson) respectively, do not therefore contain Dürrenmatt's final thoughts on the plays, as these editions have not been revised, only reprinted, since their publication in 1957 and 1966 respectively. In this book, I have indicated the most important alterations to the texts, and, after the quotations, have placed the relevant page-numbers from both editions, the older editions' numbers first, e.g. p.17/p.21. (N.B. WA7 etc. indicates Volume 7 etc. of the new *Werkausgabe*.)

It is to be hoped that the firms concerned will now consider publishing revised editions of these much studied works, if only to give students and readers the benefits of the definitive texts and of up-to-date research and bibliographies.

1. *Dürrenmatt and* Die Komödie

When Friedrich Dürrenmatt died on 14 December 1990, twenty-three days before what would have been his 70th birthday (on 5 January), the literary world mourned a writer who had always been his own man and who had never fitted into any one category. At first sight his 'Swiss-ness' would seem to have paired him with the other leading Swiss writer of his generation, Max Frisch, but in reality they had only their 'Swiss-ness' in common. Where Frisch, born in 1911 in fashionable Zürich, was a man of the world, an architect with residences outside Switzerland, Dürrenmatt, born in 1921 in the tiny village of Konolfingen, near Berne, never left Switzerland, only taking up residence (in 1952) in Neuchâtel in the Jura, in French-speaking Switzerland (known as 'Welschschweiz') where, as he often made clear, he always felt a foreigner. He wrote once of his *Wahlheimat*: 'Könnte ich "Neuenburg" sagen, hätte ich die Stadt akzeptiert, aber als "Neuchâtel" halte ich sie höflich auf Distanz...., sie ist mir nie ganz vertraut geworden' (5, p.18).

Because of the dearth of native authors in Germany immediately after the Second World War where so many had fallen in the conflict and others were still in captivity or in exile, the situation was ideal for non-German writers like Frisch and Dürrenmatt, untainted by Nazi ideological language, to fill that particular vacuum. Dürrenmatt's first play, *Es steht geschrieben*, which had its premiere on 19 March 1947, although causing a slight scandal with its rather excessive language and explicit scenes, established the twenty-six-year-old author as a literary force, and he never looked back.

Even though it is intended in the present book to discuss his two most celebrated plays, it would be inappropriate not to mention the other fields of activity in which Dürrenmatt has made a name for himself. Most students of German literature will at least have heard of his three youthful crime novels, the 'Krimis', *Der Richter und sein Henker* (WA19, 1950), *Der Verdacht* (WA19, 1953) and *Das Versprechen* (WA22, 1957). Often dismissed as 'literary potboilers', the three stories have received international acclaim, albeit mainly in schools and universities where they are in steady demand as 'set texts' and seem to catch the imagination of young students. (*Der Richter und sein Henker* alone has sold over two million copies.) Sadly, in my opinion, this success has contributed to the belief in some academic quarters that Dürrenmatt is really a rather lightweight author, suitable for A-level and *Abitur* studies, but not for consideration by serious literary critics. Those who know Dürrenmatt's complete oeuvre will be aware that he has contributed to many serious literary and political debates, not only in his dramas and novels, but in his later years especially, in a series of philosophical essays.

These essays deserve to be carefully studied, since they show us, on the one hand, why Dürrenmatt gave up writing serious dramas for the theatre, why indeed he abandoned the theatre after the failure of his play *Achterloo* in 1983, even though he wrote another version in 1988; and, on the other hand, how he has remained faithful to three or four major themes visible in all of his works. These themes relate, I believe, to issues of public and personal guilt and, in almost all of his works, we find him accusing his main characters of failings, great and small, and of conduct prejudicial to the welfare of the individual — a topos which bulks large in Dürrenmatt's work. It is his own concern with the individual and his right to be free which marks Dürrenmatt out as one of the true descendants of that philosophic age known as the 'Enlightenment', the eighteenth century, the age of such writers as David Hume in Scotland, Voltaire in France and Lessing in Germany, the century of which Bernard Le Bovier de Fontenelle prophesied in 1702 that it would 'become more enlightened day by day so that all previous centuries will be lost in darkness by comparison.' (He was writing the preface to the *History of the Renewal of the Royal Academy of Sciences*.)

Dürrenmatt's first two plays *Es steht geschrieben* (WA1, 1947) and *Der Blinde* (WA1, 1948) were the works of a typical, young, post-war intellectual, writing in a Nietzschean, God-is-dead tradition, attacking the religious tenets of his Swiss forebears. Early commentators on his work, such as Jauslin (*47*), Brock-Sulzer (*22*) and Boyd (*20*), had stressed the religious aspect of the plays. In his introduction, Jauslin, discussing the day when literary critics would be able to evaluate Dürrenmatt's *Gesamtwerk* wrote, in 1964: 'Da wäre dann vor allem die theologisch-ethische Fragestellung nicht zu umgehen' (*47*, p.7). Fritz Buri's 1962 article, *Der 'Einfall' der Gnade in Dürrenmatts dramatischem Werk* (*23*, pp.35-69), had already given students of Dürrenmatt the leitmotiv for their essays, dissertations and lectures. Dürrenmatt's obvious interest in theological matters was however to be seen by later critics as more an expression of his feelings of guilt at having abandoned the faith of his parents (see below, p.71). More important to Dürrenmatt has been his interest in international politics; from *Romulus der Große* onward (WA2, 1949) his plays have concerned themselves with the moral and ethical problems resulting from the clash of the two great twentieth-century ideologies: capitalism and communism. His insistence on the individual's right to freedom, his hatred of dogmatism and single-issue fanatics, led to his taking issue in his plays, novels, stories and essays with the horrors perpetrated in Korea, Vietnam, Hungary, Suez, Biafra, Czechoslovakia and the Gulf, where both ideologies seemed to him to be furthering a dehumanization of mankind and the spoliation of his environment.

Dürrenmatt's early works seemed to these commentators to reflect his youthful background, the son of deeply religious parents: the father a Calvinist clergyman in a small Swiss village, the mother a typically conservative, religious Swiss of peasant descent. The move to the 'big town', Berne, the Swiss capital, in 1933 when the author was twelve, gave Dürrenmatt his first taste of the Switzerland known to the rest of the world: rich, complacent and, above all, politically neutral. These three factors have concerned Swiss intellectuals at all times and have conditioned their attitudes and their writings, yet it was really only in the post-war years that 'writers began to challenge the national myths nurtured by a profoundly conservative society' (*25*, p.2).

It was only when he began his studies of German literature and philosophy at the universities of Zürich and Berne in 1941 that Dürrenmatt was able to break away from his cloistered family environment and to begin to replace his former reading of Swiss myths and battles of long ago with more directed and scholarly reading of the classics of German and world literature. In *Rollenspiele* (*3*) Dürrenmatt recalls the composition of his first story *Weihnacht*, written on Christmas Eve 1942 in Zürich after a rather wild drinking session. It would, of course, be foolhardy to claim that a writer's very first story pointed 'the way forward', but the reader of *Der Besuch der alten Dame* in particular, who has smiled over the author's cynical presentation of 'Der Pfarrer' might think that these 122 words do have some future significance:

> Es war Weihnacht. Ich ging über die weite Ebene. Der Schnee war wie Glas. Es war kalt. Die Luft war tot. Keine Bewegung, kein Ton. Der Horizont war rund. Der Himmel schwarz. Die Sterne gestorben. Der Mond gestern zu Grabe getragen. Die Sonne nicht aufgegangen. Ich schrie. Ich hörte mich nicht. Ich schrie wieder. Ich sah einen Körper auf dem Schnee liegen. Es war das Christkind. Die Glieder weiß und starr. Der Heiligenschein eine gelbe gefrorene Scheibe. Ich nahm das Kind in die Hände. Ich bewegte seine Arme auf und ab. Ich hatte Hunger. Ich aß den Heiligenschein. Er schmeckte wie altes Brot. Ich biß ihm den Kopf ab. Alter Marzipan. Ich ging weiter. (WA18, pp.9-12).

Such short, laconic sentences were to become one of the hallmarks of Dürrenmatt's later prose style.[1] However, he himself

---

[1] In his plays Dürrenmatt marries this laconic style with the Greek comedy convention known as *stichomythia* where the characters speak in single lines (in Greek, usually rhymed). We meet this form first of all in Act I of *Der*

later admitted that the 'style' arose mainly from his own lack of command of correct, literary German (*Hochdeutsch*), since, like most Swiss Germans, his native tongue was that of his region, in his case, the Bernese Oberland, which is called *Landberndeutsch*; literary German had had to be learned as a foreign language. Dürrenmatt's day-to-day language was therefore always this 'Schwyzertütsch' which, as we shall see later, had a considerable influence on the writing of *Der Besuch der alten Dame*.

'Es galt gegen die Welt an sich zu protestieren, Gott an sich zu attackieren,' wrote Dürrenmatt later about this period of his life (in *Labyrinth, 8*, p.292), and we therefore feel inclined to treat this very short story as a pointer to the future, since almost all of Dürrenmatt's future works inveigh against one or other symbol of the Swiss 'establishment' — that conservative, rather smug group of rich Swiss in the 'playground of Europe', whose financial acumen has led to their being described, rather sardonically, as the 'gnomes of Zürich'. Here, in this short story, the attack is against the powerful Protestant Church Establishment which was later to denounce so roundly his first two plays. Elisabeth Brock-Sulzer defended the young dramatist in her review of the premiere of *Es steht geschrieben* and his right to shock 'unser allzu friedlich die Kunst und ihr Gegenteil verdauendes Publikum' (22).

Among dramatists whom the twenty-two-year-old student read in Berne and Zürich was the Greek comic writer Aristophanes (c.445-c.386 B.C.) whose earthy, witty yet cruel comedies (e.g. *The Birds, The Frogs, The Wasps* and *The Clouds*) gave Dürrenmatt the idea for a comic style which he then made his own. In an essay *Anmerkung zur Komödie* of 1952, he wrote: 'Diese Komödien [i.e. of Aristophanes] sind Eingriffe in die Wirklichkeit' (WA24, p.21); these 'encroachments into reality' concerned not the people of past ages, but of Aristophanes' own times: the statesmen, philosophers, poets and generals; and this is what Dürrenmatt wanted from his *Komödien*. (It is necessary to distinguish in German between *Komödie* and *Lustspiel*: the first is more realistic and, at times,

---

Besuch der alten Dame where the five Bürger are describing the decrepit state of Güllen.

crueller than its merely funny, harmless companion, the *Lustspiel*. Otto Rommel drew this distinction most sharply when he wrote:

> das Lustspiel ist so ein Stück, wenn es gelingt, die Problematik des Lebens [...] in das Licht einer heiteren Gelöstheit zu rücken bzw. durch die Fiktion einer dramatischen Handlung ein solches Gefühl zu erzeugen. Die Komödie dagegen ist beherrscht durch die 'komische Gestalt', die im Lichte des absteigenden Kontrastes gesehen wird; in ihr wird durch alle Lustigkeit hindurch doch meist die Schärfe satirischen Zorns oder die Bitterkeit der Ohnmacht fühlbar,... *(70*, p.273)

The 'acerbity of satirical anger' and the 'bitter feeling of powerlessness' can be found in all of Dürrenmatt's works.)

Dürrenmatt believed that, by making his plays *Komödien*, he gained a number of advantages: firstly, he could distance his characters, make them 'Gleichnisse der menschlichen Situation' (WA24, p.23), so that his audience, while appreciating the contemporaneity of the character types, would also be aware that what they were witnessing was a description of human follies which have always existed — and which always will exist — and that, by laughing at these follies, they might help to rid these people of their power. Secondly, Dürrenmatt saw in the Aristophanic comedy the power of the grotesque, that literary device often known as 'deformation' or what F.G. Jünger termed the 'Haß gegen das Schöne' (cf. *51*, p.13), which, as Arnold Heidsieck put it, was a deformation of reality 'von einer Art, die den Betrachter entsetzt und zugleich lachen macht, die grauenvoll und lächerlich in eins ist' (*41*, p.15). It is this element indeed which, as I have already hinted, differentiates the *Komödie* from the *Lustspiel* by dehumanizing the characters of the play and perverting reality; the audience freezes with apprehension or horror, yet must laugh at the same time. There are few Dürrenmatt plays in which the grotesque does not make an appearance, either in the characters (Claire or Dr von Zahnd) or in the stage action (the Konradsweilerwald scene, or the meal at the end of *Die Physiker*). (See too below, p.27.)

After the Second World War, Dürrenmatt believed with many other writers that the age was 'too serious for tragedies'; the world had become so perilous that one could only laugh at the disorder; man was adrift in a world alien to his normal ways, unable to make sense of it all. One will recall that this was, of course, the age of the Cold War and the constant threat of The Bomb, a threat which hung over Dürrenmatt's world throughout his career as a writer.

George Steiner in his *The Death of Tragedy* (1961) wrote that tragedy as the Greeks knew it was dead. The very meaning of Greek tragedy, of an Oedipus or an Antigone, rested on the belief in an ineluctable fate, in *ananké*. Since the tragic vision demanded the unconditional acceptance of one's destiny, the outcome was final, there could be no Happy End. 'Tragedies end badly,' wrote Steiner memorably (*75*, pp.8 and 129). The hero, through some fault (*hamartia*) in his nature, fell from his high estate, invoking pity and fear in the hearts of the audience. If our age could no longer produce that, what should replace it?

Dürrenmatt argued that if 'pure tragedy' could no longer be written in this age of shifting moral values, then perhaps the 'tragic element' ('das Tragische') might still be produced: 'Wir können das Tragische *aus der Komödie* [my italics] heraus erzielen, hervorbringen als einen schrecklichen Moment, als einen sich öffnenden Abgrund' (in *Theaterprobleme*, 1954/55, WA24, p.63). And it is this 'yawning chasm' which regularly opens up in a Dürrenmatt *Komödie* making the audience (or the reader) pause — and perhaps gasp — at the paradoxical twist in the tale. And the paradox is closely linked to another Dürrenmattian trademark, perfectly explained in Point 9 of *Die Physiker*:

> Planmäßig vorgehende Menschen wollen ein bestimmtes Ziel erreichen. Der Zufall trifft sie dann am schlimmsten, wenn sie durch ihn das Gegenteil ihres Ziels erreichen: Das, was sie befürchteten, was sie zu vermeiden suchten (z.B. Oedipus).

The concept *Zufall* is an ever-present one in Dürrenmatt's work. It is chance which limits man and his ability to plan his life, for it shows that there is an incalculable element in life which can make a mockery of our puny human efforts; Timo Tiusanen calls chance ' a gap in the chain of logic' (*76*, p.86), and Dürrenmatt invites us continually to laugh to scorn those who affect to ignore this gap.

That his works castigate human weaknesses through laughter is undoubtedly true, and this has led some commentators, such as Jan Knopf, to regard the author as a 'black pessimist' who sees only the ills of the world, and men's actions as dastardly. Knopf compares Dürrenmatt's pessimism with Brecht's optimism. He writes:

> erkennt Dürrenmatt in der menschlichen Geschichte nur Destruktion, so legt Brecht ihre produktiven, veränderlichen Dimensionen frei; wo bei Dürrenmatt der Tod nistet, beginnt bei Brecht das Leben — und zwar immer wieder und stets neu.   (*60*, p.189)

This is why the socialist Knopf summed up most of Dürrenmatt's work as 'konservativer Kulturpessimismus', but that was written in the past.[2] I prefer to see Dürrenmatt as a realist who understands the nature of the beast, and who realizes that, *pace* Brecht, man will never change, that evil will always be with us, but that, by showing the dangers for what they are, there is just a chance that evil will not always triumph. That is why there is in almost every Dürrenmatt work one character who tries not to despair, but to make a stand against the worst possible turn of the plot and to attempt, as Dürrenmatt puts it, 'die Welt zu bestehen'. In *Theaterprobleme*, Dürrenmatt called such people 'mutige Menschen' who, by their actions, had 'die verlorene Weltordnung wieder hergestellt' (WA24, p.63), 'courageous people' who, by not despairing, had managed to restore to their world some sort of order which, of course, included this element of absurd and blind chance.

Thus we see all of Dürrenmatt's works as warnings; at their weakest they can become semi-religious moral tracts (like *Die Ehe*

---

[2]Knopf, J., *Friedrich Dürrenmatt* (München, Beck, 1976), p.106.

des Herrn Mississippi of 1952, WA3) 'pointing a moral and adorning a tale', as Samuel Johnson wrote in his *Charles XII of Sweden*. At their best, and my chosen two plays are among that best, they put over a powerful case for our consideration: in *Der Besuch der alten Dame* we are shown the evils of the love of money, the evils of greed and personal dishonesty; in *Die Physiker*, we see the results of overweening selfishness when a group of people believe that *their* work is more important than the good of society.

It would be misleading to claim that Dürrenmatt remained throughout his life true to his belief in the ability of men 'die Welt zu bestehen'. In later works, particularly in those which he wrote after he felt that he had been rejected by the world of the theatre, as for instance after the failure of *Der Mitmacher* (WA14, 1973), there is undoubtedly a strain of pessimism to be found, not unconnected with the increasingly severe effects of the diabetes from which he had suffered since his youth. His first heart attacks in 1969 and 1975 and the loss, in 1983, of his first wife Lotti to whom he had been married for thirty-seven years, no doubt also contributed to this growing pessimism. And yet in 1984 Dürrenmatt remarried, and with his new wife, Charlotte Kerr, a film-maker from Munich, produced several new works, including his play *Achterloo* which, although he wrote some seven versions (the last appearing as *Achterloo IV* at the Schwetzingen Festival in 1988), did not restore his reputation as a leading European playwright.

However, when reading, studying or watching *Der Besuch der alten Dame* and *Die Physiker*, one must not forget that they were written and produced in 1956 and 1962 respectively and that they were therefore conceived in the age and spirit of that essay *Theaterprobleme* of 1954-55. Thus, although I would agree that both plays are in Dürrenmatt's words 'Gleichnisse der menschlichen Situation' and that these themes are therefore timeless and transcend the date of their composition, they cannot be fully understood without some knowledge of their genesis against the background of their times; and it is to this that I now turn.

2. Der Besuch der alten Dame: *The* Einfall — *Genesis and Development*

In the essay *Theaterprobleme* to which I have already referred, Dürrenmatt writes of the 'Einfall' which is the central element of his (and Aristophanes') *Komödien* and which distinguishes them from tragedies, because it is the 'Einfall', that 'happy idea', as the old Greek comedy called it, which distances audiences by making them laugh happily at what later will turn out to be deadly serious. Tragedy, the author claims, makes the audience identify too closely with the events in the play, thus making critical appraisal difficult. Clearly Dürrenmatt approaches here Brecht's principle of 'Verfremdung', translated usually into French as ' distantiation', but into English as 'alienation'. Both authors saw their theatre as one of confrontation, Brecht in rather more politicized terms than the Swiss who believed that he was creating something other than a mere representation of the present world and its ills; he believed that he was creating a 'Gegenwelt', an alternative world, in which, as he wrote in No. 39 of his *46 Sätze über das Theater* of 1970, 'die Wirklichkeit [ist] die Unwahrscheinlichkeit, die eingetreten ist' (WA24, p.205). His plays tell us therefore of improbabilities which, through chance, have become realities — and these are the unexpected realities which confront his audience.

How Dürrenmatt found and developed his 'Einfälle' was only revealed to the literary world with the publication of the two volumes *Stoffe I* and *Stoffe II-III* in 1981. These books of memoirs, now together entitled *Labyrinth* (8), give personal information about the genesis of his works. We read, for example, of a holiday which he spent in a little village in the Bernese Oberland when he was a university student in Berne in 1941. Sitting in the village pub listening to the locals' rather wild and unbelievable ghost stories,

Dürrenmatt was fascinated by one which told of the former landlord's encounter with a gigantic snow-white wolfhound at midnight by full moon in a nearby wood, the Stinkhaldenwald, as a result of which the landlord died of fright six days later. Dürrenmatt was likewise seized with panic when he had to cycle through this wood at midnight, daring the ghostly wolfhound to come to him, and then crashing back through the wood, bathed in sweat.

His plots, Dürrenmatt wrote in that same volume, often arise from 'Erinnerungen, die sich im Unbewußten mit einem Einfall verbunden haben' and both of these then become a mixture of 'Erleben, Phantasie und Stoff' (*8*, p.221). The full moon had already played a role in a prank of his early days in Berne when one night he and some friends, rather drunk, kept telephoning the Meteorological Institute of the university to tell them that there was something wrong with the shape of the full moon. Apart from giving him a life-long interest in astronomy, this comic experience, united with his memories of his holiday in the mountain village, produced the germ of a story which he later published in that volume of reminiscences. The story is entitled *Mondfinsternis*, meaning 'eclipse of the moon' (*8*, pp.232-80) and its locale is the Bernese Oberland where Dürrenmatt spent that holiday in 1941. Although the story is printed in *Hochdeutsch*, it is plain, if only from the names of the characters, that Dürrenmatt had thought it out in his own dialect of *Landberndeutsch*.

The tale begins in the depths of winter in a tiny Emmental village, Flötenbach, high up in the mountains and separated from the larger village, Flötigen, by a steep road, practically impassable in winter. There arrives in Flötigen a burly, six-foot tall *Auslandschweizer*, Walt Lotcher, returned from Canada to his native village. He drives an equally large Cadillac up the mountain road, eventually collides with a telegraph pole and sticks fast in metre-deep snow. After stumbling over a frozen corpse, he reaches the Hotel-Gasthof Bären, and it is immediately obvious that he recognizes the landlord — the successor to that frozen corpse! He is now the *Gemeindepräsident* (the mayor), Schlaginhaufens Seppu. (In this region, the Christian name comes second, as in Hungarian. The young Dürrenmatt was always known to his neighbours in Konolfingen as 'Pfarrers Fritzli' ('Parson's little Freddie').)

From the mayor, Walt — once known locally as Lochers Wauti, then as Walt Lotcher in Canada — learns that the girl with whom he had fallen in love, Kläri Zurbriggen, had married the man for whom she had spurned Walt forty years earlier, but that she had also borne Walt's child, and that boy, Döufu Jöggu, is now still living with Kläri and her husband, Döufu Mani. Walt learns too that the village has been left behind in the economic race and that only the stupid ones — 'arm wie Kirchenmäuse' — have not left for a better life. Walt tells the landlord of the land that he owns in Canada, 'größer als das Berner Oberland', and suddenly asks how many households there are in the village: sixteen is the answer, including the woman teacher and the policeman, who, however, are not from the village. Walt tells the landlord that he will leave each family (excluding the teacher and the policeman) a million — if they will kill Döufu Mani: 'Ich habe einst geschworen, mich zu rächen, ich erinnere mich jetzt auf einmal, und den Schwur halte ich,' he says (*8*, p.237), although he cannot quite remember whether he wanted revenge on Kläri or on Mani.

While the landlord/mayor calls the villagers together (and also arranges to rescue Walt's car with the fourteen million of cash), Walt installs himself upstairs with a plentiful supply of schnaps, beer and a succession of the local girls. Sure that the chance of a lifetime to save the village has arrived, the mayor and the village men begin their discussion. Mani is allowed to speak first ('sie seien schließlich eine Demokratie,' says the landlord, *8*, p.243) and, surprisingly, he raises no objection to being killed: 'das Leben mache ihm sowieso längst keinen Spaß mehr,' he says; but before they can continue, one of the village girls appears, naked, from Walt's room to inform them that the millionaire does not want Mani to die until the next full moon, i.e. in ten days' time. Carefully, Dürrenmatt shows how the various villagers, particularly the younger ones, begin to calculate how much money each could receive and how, in so doing, old family resentments (and secrets) are awakened.

While Mani leaves the room, the suggestion is made that the death must be made to look like an accident and, in a superbly comic passage, we learn how Mani should be killed by an axe while sitting under a special beech, the 'Blüttlibuche', which should then be felled on top of him; the wood should be welcomed by the parson for the beams of the church roof! A slight panic arises when Mani returns to say that he has changed his mind, but only that he wants to visit the agricultural show on the Saturday before the full moon in order to show his two sons the best farm implements to buy with their money. Off they all go to the show in the village of Oberlottikofen, and there, guided by an 'aristocratic' *Auslandschweizer*, Benno von Lafrigen, they watch the most up-to-date method of removing cow dung from the stalls and letting it run away as liquid manure (called in Swiss German 'die Gülle') into the gutters outside the town.

While the villagers are drowning their boredom in a variety of taverns, the regional councillors come to ask Herr Schlaginhaufen why his village refuses to clear the snow from their steep mountain road. When he still refuses to co-operate, they tell him that they will do the job for him and will send him the bill. Nobody in Oberlottikofen knows about Walt's offer, of course, so when one of the councillors feels that he must defend the villagers' wish not 'to dance round the Golden Calf', but to retain their own old traditions and the beauty of their village, the Dürrenmattian paradox is delightfully comical.

As they stagger back to the village on the Sunday morning, blind drunk like fans from a football match, the villagers are suddenly confronted by the clergyman who had had to climb up through the snow to take his monthly service. The mayor promises to cut down the beech that very night as a reward for the church. 'Eine christliche Tat,' says the hypocritical clergyman who is himself a follower of the 'new' religion, 'eine Theologie ohne Gott', and whom we shall find later making illicit love to the schoolmistress and organist, Claudine Zäpfel.

When Kläri, Mani's wife, hears of their intent, she will have nothing to do with the idea, or with the money. She married Mani, she says, because he was an honest man who married her even though she was pregnant by another man; she knew that she could never have relied on Walt Lotcher, and now she has been proved right. Lotcher simply wants to have a joke at their expense, she says, because he despises them all, but her Mani will be the one to suffer. Mani refuses to listen to her and the villagers sit him under the selected beech. But Mani suddenly points out that the full moon is no longer full: an eclipse, a 'Mondfinsternis', has begun and one of the superstitious villagers is of the opinion that this is why Walt Lotcher has insisted on a murder on the night of the full moon: 'die Erde und die Welt werden untergehen' (*8*, p.269). This scene, with Dürrenmatt's superbly ghostly description of the vanishing moon, reaches comical greatness as the villagers pray in terror. But as the moon reappears, fear vanishes, the beech is felled and Mani lies dead, 'schön zerquetscht [...] ein einziger Brei' (*8*, p.271).

On the news of Mani's death, Lotcher prepares to leave, while the mayor rushes up to the bedroom to count the money and tries to ignore his wife, lying naked in Lotcher's bed; but the other women, along with his wife, remind him that they are all now millionaires and that they do not intend to do any more work. It is only as Lotcher's Cadillac drives away that he meets Kläri for the first time in forty years: she is going down to Oberlottikofen to seek work. Walt confesses to her that he had never given his native village a thought until he had been struck by a heart attack, and in bed in Canada he was overcome by a desire to see the village and the wood again. When he heard that Kläri had had his child, he was seized by a 'Riesenwut', but this 'monstrous anger', Walt suggests, might only have been a great longing to relive the days of his youth, and he would probably have given the village the money even had no one been killed. Kläri is full of self-contempt, as is Walt, and she gets out of the car to walk down to the station on her own. But as she leaves Walt and he tries to drive off, he is stricken once more by a heart attack and ends up as he began: stuck in the deep snow, but this time dead.

A comical postlude tells how the teacher, leaving her sleeping clergyman lover, tries to make her way back up the village road and is helped by the regional councillors who have come with an army of men in orange anoraks to clear the road. 'Es sei Aufgabe der Gemeinschaft,' they tell the mayor, 'ihr hartes Los hier oben zu lindern' (8, p.279) and that they will now erect a 'Winter-Vita-Parcours-Zentrum' for the tourists: ten million from the federal government, five million from the canton and twenty-five million from the insurance. Amazed at the turn of events, for he had believed that the men had come to charge them all with murder, the mayor can only murmur hypocritically as he fingers the money: 'wir danken dir, Gott hat uns gesegnet' (8, p.280).

It is instructive for the student of literature to follow the thought processes of an author as he expands an idea, a poem or a short story into a longer literary form. It also, at times, explains the psychological treatment of the characters and milieu of the final art form. In his discussion of *Mondfinsternis* in *Labyrinth* Dürrenmatt admitted that his first thought had been to abandon the chapter on the mountain village, but then he realized that it contained motifs which, with other autobiographical memories, had led directly to the writing of *Der Besuch der alten Dame* (8, pp.230-32). I will now consider four of these:

1) The basic milieu is a desolate, run-down Swiss village, miles from anywhere, locked into its mediaeval superstitions and traditions, its lack of contact with the wider world underscored by the super-Helvetic names: Mani, Döufu, Migger Hacker, Nobi Geißgraser, Res Stierer et al. The village's name is Flötenbach, but Dürrenmatt, on re-reading his story, immediately saw the potential of a remark he had one of his characters make when the villagers visited the agricultural show in Oberlottikofen and heard the heel-clicking von Lafrigen explain, in *Hochdeutsch* and at some length, how the cattle dung and urine mixed with straw were cleverly led out into the 'Güllengrube': 'Es sei Zeit, den Schwätzer selber in die Gülle zu spülen' (8, p.250), says one of the bored villagers in *Oberländerdeutsch* — and here was the perfect name for the village in the play: Güllen, for a Bernese Swiss, an unpleasant stinking hole, connected here to High German pretentiousness.

It only took Dürrenmatt's memories of the journeys that he made between Neuchâtel and Berne (some twenty miles) in 1953, when his wife had fallen seriously ill shortly before the Munich premiere of his play *Ein Engel kommt nach Babylon*, and of the stops that even express trains made at the two tiny insignificant stations of Ins and Kerzers, to give shape to the very first scene of the play.

2) Dürrenmatt wrote *Mondfinsternis* after one of these journeys in 1953 and he freely admits that the decision to turn the story into a play was — at first anyway — a purely financial one: 'Ich sah darin eine bessere Möglichkeit, Geld zu verdienen, als mit dem Schreiben einer Novelle' (*8*, p.230). Yet the theme of revenge which runs through the play like a red thread is treated very lightly in the story. True, Walt Lotcher returns to the village as Claire does in the play, but when asked by the mayor on whom he wants to wreak revenge, he can only answer: 'Vergessen [...] nur daß ich mich rächen muß, weil ich es geschworen habe, habe ich nicht vergessen' (*8*, p.237). This is far away from the brooding, sinister remarks of Claire at the banquet at the end of Act I of the play. She has had the desire for revenge simmering in her since her ignominious departure from Güllen as a seventeen-year-old girl, and somehow her revenge is much more single-minded. Walt's departure, as he admits to Kläri at the end, was caused more by his disgust for 'dieses Land und das übrige blöde Europa' (*8*, p.273), and this disgust is now compounded by the disgust that he feels for his life since leaving the village; his shady financial deals which have made him disgustingly rich, his many love affairs and his son who is an even bigger rogue than Walt himself. He admits that he had completely forgotten about her Mani, the village and everyone in it. Thus, the request to kill Mani seems to have been an impulse. Certainly, as we have seen, he admits to Kläri right at the end of the story, that it was not really anger that made him demand Mani's death, but rather a longing ('eine ungeheure Gier [...] noch einmal zu leben', *8*, p.274), when he realized that his heart attacks were going eventually to prove fatal.

3) Dürrenmatt has explained in many interviews and articles since 1956 why the main character in *Mondfinsternis* was transmogrified into the female Claire Zachanassian in the play (see *66*, p.14 and *19*, pp.107-08). The reason was not, he now insists, to make a major role for one of his favourite actresses, the German,

Therese Giehse, but rather to make the whole play much more theatrical ('bühnenatmosphärisch' was his term). The idea of a someone coming in from outside to right a wrong is a very old theatrical and filmic device: keen filmgoers will recall Alan Ladd in *Shane*, and many other heroes (usually dressed all in black) riding into the hick town to seek revenge and justice. Claire's femininity in the role doubled this eeriness in 1956. Walt's thwarted arrival in the deep snow was intensified later by news of his impending heart attack; Claire's arrival in a sedan chair is later intensified by her description of how she lost her limbs in an air accident over Afghanistan, and Dürrenmatt then sought to combine this dramatic idea with his memories (his 'Erlebnis') of his train stopping at the little stations Ins and Kerzers to justify the billionairess' arriving by train.

Dürrenmatt's relationships to his women characters have always been worthy of examination; the majority of them are what we call 'grotesques': women with some element of comic monstrosity about them. The two most famous are Claire Zachanassian and Dr Mathilde von Zahnd, of course, but students of Dürrenmatt's works will no doubt recall Dr Edith Marlok in *Der Verdacht* (WA19), Anastasia Mississippi in *Die Ehe des Herrn Mississippi* (WA3), Ottilie Frank in *Frank V* (WA6), Alice, the wife, in *Play Strindberg* (WA12) and many more. Had we not known that Dürrenmatt had been happily married for thirty-seven years to one woman, Lotti Geißler, and then, on her unexpected death in 1983, to Charlotte Kerr in 1984 till his own death in 1990, we might reasonably have suspected him of misogyny, but all these characters play the role assigned to the grotesque by Dürrenmatt in that early essay *Anmerkung zur Komödie* where he posits two forms of the grotesque: one, known from Romantic literature, which tries to awake 'Furcht oder absonderliche Gefühle', and another introduced for the purpose of distancing, 'die *nur* durch dieses Mittel zu schaffen ist' (WA24, p.24). Dürrenmatt could imagine the Second World War being treated in a grotesque manner on the stage, but not played as a tragedy, since we were not yet distanced enough from it: he was writing, of course, in 1952. The grotesque, he went on, is not the art of the nihilist — that was the charge in these days — but rather the art of the moralist; it was a matter 'des Witzes und des scharfen Verstandes [...] unbequem aber nötig' (WA24, pp.24-25).

The theme of the grotesque was then to occupy the attention of writers on Dürrenmatt for many years to come. Indeed, he became the 'playwright of the grotesque' (cf. Diller, _27/28_, Helbling, _42-44_, and Reed, _67_). Wolfgang Kayser's book _Das Groteske_ (_52_) defined it as a subspecies of the comic in aesthetic theories and demonstrated how it had come to mirror man's failure to orientate himself in the physical universe: 'Die Gestaltungen des Grotesken sind der lauteste und sinnfälligste Widerspruch gegen jeden Rationalismus und gegen jede Systematik des Denkens' (p.202), and although I believe, with Kayser, that the grotesque is more relevant to the visual arts, his definition does lend support to Dürrenmatt's dramaturgical application of the grotesque and chance in his work.

4) The sacrifice of Mani is rather underplayed compared to the moral decision reached by Ill in the play. Mani, disgusted with the decay and desolation in Flötenbach, does not seem to fear death, indeed, he almost volunteers for it, and the death scene itself is, as I have said, a fine example of comic description. However, the germ, the true _Einfall_, of Alfred's murder by the hypocritical villagers of Güllen does lie there and is extended in the play to include Alfred's expiation for having despoiled Claire. That Alfred's death should be described as a heart attack by the doctor mirrors Walt's own condition and makes this means of death one of Dürrenmatt's favourite ploys — and a grim prophecy of his second major heart attack in October 1975, so vividly described in the essay _Wie die Frist entstand_ (WA15, pp.135-47), and the cause of his own death in 1990. The figure of Death is rarely absent from Dürrenmatt's writings; indeed, Hans Mayer criticized him for the 'Leichenberge' left on the stage at the end of his earlier plays (see _62_, p.105); as he grew older and had himself faced death on several occasions during his severe illnesses, and, above all, when he found his wife lying dead in their house on 16 January 1983, it did seem that he realized how important a role it had played in his work; to begin with, it was

what Northrop Frye called 'the ritual death of comedy',[3] best exemplified by the 'regular deaths' of Wolfgang Schwitter in Dürrenmatt's *Der Meteor* of 1966 (WA9); but then in that late essay *Abschied vom Theater* written on 21 November 1990, three weeks before his death, Dürrenmatt wrote: 'Vielleicht ist der Tod der Vater aller Dinge' (*11*, p.186) and went on to suggest of these grotesque figures in his works: 'Sie alle nehmen in meinem Welttheater die Stelle Gottes ein', since he could not picture a Christian God, but only a God of our times who had become, like these characters, 'eine Groteske'.

---

[3]*The Anatomy of Criticism* (Princeton, Princeton University Press, 1957), p.179.

3. Der Besuch der alten Dame: *The Play and its Minor Characters*

When the first full commentaries on *Der Besuch der alten Dame* appeared, it was suggested in many of them that the play had clear Expressionist traits, not just on stylistic grounds, but also because many of the characters had no names: they were designated simply as 'Der Erste', 'Der Zweite', 'Der Bürgermeister' etc. True, they are so designated in the *Personenliste*, but a close reading of the text reveals that many of them are in fact named, and named in a very significant fashion. The naming of characters to suggest their personalities and/or characteristics has a very long history, reaching back into Greek times. There we find stereotyped characters in the comedy: 'the unresourceful young lover, the testy old father, the indulgent mother [...] the parasite, the impudent slave, the bragging soldier' (*39*, p.318). Aristophanes, whom, as we have seen, Dürrenmatt often took as his model, was a past master of the art; think of the titles of his plays, *The Knights*, *The Frogs*, *The Wasps*, *The Clouds*: all satirical references to the personal faults of the societies depicted within; then the generalized characters: Strepsiades (literally, the 'Debt-Dodger') and Pheidomides ('Parsimonious') in *The Clouds*; Pisthetairos ('The Plausible One'), a pushing rogue, in *The Birds* and, more obviously perhaps, Procleon and Anticleon, the two characters in *The Wasps* who demonstrate the two views held of the demagogue Cleon, Aristophanes' *bête noire*. In German literature, Frank Wedekind (1864-1918) was a favourite writer of Dürrenmatt's; in the play *Frühlings Erwachen* (1891) Wedekind named his vindictive schoolteachers Affenschmalz, Knüppeldick, Knochenbruch and Fliegentod, while, in English literature, we find the device most clearly demonstrated by Charles Dickens: Dotheboys Hall, a tyrannical boys' school, in *Nicholas*

Nickleby; Sir Leicester Deadlock, a pompous baronet, in *Bleak House*; Mr Gradgrind, a cruel industrialist, in *Hard Times* and many others. In the last resort, authors who use this device are attempting to point a moral, to chastise with laughter, to bring down those who think themselves better than others, or whose means of becoming better than others were, at best dubious, at worst criminal. As Aristophanes wrote in Act II of *The Frogs*: 'From the very earliest times, the really great poet has been the one who had a useful lesson to teach.'

Dürrenmatt has used this device throughout his career, wittily, sarcastically, even cruelly. In his very first play, *Es steht geschrieben*, the monk who fights to save his skin is called Maximilian Bleibeganz; the prostitute in *Der Blinde* is Gräfin Freudenberg (a house of ill repute in German is 'ein Freudenhaus'); the main character in *Romulus der Große* is based on the name of the last Roman Emperor, Romulus Augustulus, i.e. Augustus the Little, but altered sarcastically in the play to Romulus the Great (or the Big); in *Der Meteor*, the name of the critic is based on the names of two of Dürrenmatt's least favourite Germans, Stefan George, the poet, and Friedrich Gundolf, the critic, and the names become Friedrich Georgen. In *Der Richter und sein Henker* the main character, Alfredo Traps, takes his name from the Swiss-German noun 'ein Trappi', a fellow who is prone to accidents. In an interview that I had with Dürrenmatt several years ago, he said: 'Es gibt alle Arten von Namen, erfundene Namen und vorhandene Namen' as well as 'versteckt erfundene Namen', and we can see that most of the names chosen for his characters do represent a function which helps us to understand his or her characterization in the work.[4]

We can now turn to the characters in *Der Besuch der alten Dame* and examine their characteristics in the light of these remarks. A study of the *Personenliste* shows that the characters there can be

---

[4]See 77. He did warn us, however, not to 'search in vain'; the celebrated name 'Tschanz', for example, in *Der Richter und sein Henker* has set many a commentator off on the wrong track and into a discourse on the English word 'chance'. It is, Dürrenmatt assured us, a not uncommon Swiss name.

divided into three groups: the minor characters, Alfred Ill and Claire Zachanassian.

The minor characters can be subdivided firstly into those who affect the action directly: Ill's family, the Mayor, the Clergyman, the Teacher, the Doctor and the Policeman; and secondly the bystanders, Citizens I-IV, the Painter, the three women and Claire's strange retinue, and lastly, those who simply supply local colour, the Stationmaster and the Pressmen.

We learn from the conversation between Alfred and Claire in the Konradsweilerwald (pp.37-43/pp.35-40) that Alfred married Mathilde Blumhard 'mit ihrem Kleinwarenladen' after he had betrayed Claire and she had left the town. Frau Ill is portrayed as the epitome of the petite bourgeoise; when Claire is introduced to her again at the banquet in Act I, she addresses her patronisingly as 'Mathildchen' and only remembers 'wie du hinter der Ladentüre auf Alfred lauertest', but now she has become skinny and pale (p.45/p.41). Frau Ill seems to show concern for Ill when she rushes to comfort him after Claire has pronounced her demands for Alfred's death (pp.57-59/p.49), but when Act II begins, we learn that she has taken to her bed. Ill believes that she is just tired, but we guess that she is beginning to anticipate her life of gilded leisure after years of genteel poverty with Alfred.

We meet her again at the beginning of Act III when the course of the plot has become clearer. There she stands behind her shiny new counter with its new till and expensive goods, serving high-class items to the townsfolk and receiving their hypocritical condolences on the life that she has had to share with Ill, the seducer of an innocent young girl. We see that she has thrown in her lot with the Güllener and expects to benefit richly from her husband's death. Dürrenmatt fills her dialogue with cynical asides to show her shallowness of character, as when she agrees with the inquisitive pressmen that Alfred only went with Claire until he met Mathilde, when 'true love' hit him (p.127/pp.96-97).

The children, Karl and Ottilie, only really come into the action at the family outing in Act III. In 1954-56, tennis was still an upper-class game in Germany and Switzerland: there had been as yet no

Boris or Steffi to encourage the ordinary boy or girl to take up what was then a very expensive sport. Thus, the combination of Ottilie's posh name which recalled Goethe's character in his novel *Die Wahlverwandtschaften* for many, and her tennis lessons about which her father clearly knows nothing (cf. p.139/p.104), would underline for the contemporary audience how Frau Ill and her children had already deserted Alfred. Karl has also bought a 'modest' Opel Olympia — 'die sind nicht so teuer' (p.139/p.104), and, despite being unemployed, has managed, as has Ottilie, to take driving lessons. Alfred has found Frau Ill's fur coat which, she claims, she only has 'zur Ansicht', and although she is terrified that the villagers will see that she too has gone along with the general hypocrisy, she has to agree to a drive in the new car (pp.147-53/pp.109-12).

So, with Frau Ill in her Persian fur coat and Ottilie in a daring red dress, they set out in symbolic fashion, with the car represented by four chairs, on the journey which is a masterpiece of comic description. We (and Alfred) are shown how the town is rejuvenating itself with the promise of Claire's billions. Interjections from the family show their attitude to it all: Ottilie's disgust at the number of Messerschmidt cars in the village is typified by her 'C'est terrible', from which we learn, incidentally, that she is also taking (expensive) French (and English) lessons; Karl notices the new fast-food place going up which he will no doubt soon frequent; and when Alfred notices how smoothly the car takes the hill up which he had always to labour on foot, Frau Ill ignores him and rejoices in her fur coat which will keep her warm.

The supreme irony is that the journey ends at the Konradsweilerwald where Alfred gets out, the family go on to a cinema in Kalberstadt, and the second scene between Claire and Alfred is about to take place, where Alfred will learn that his fate is sealed.

In the *Anmerkung* attached to the original version, printed in English as 'Nachwort' in the Routledge edition, the author writes of the Ill family: 'Nur die Familie redet sich bis zum Schlusse ein, es komme noch alles gut, auch sie ist nicht böse, nur schwach wie alle' (p.189/p.144). Of course, whether they were *just* weak is a moral question which each reader or spectator will probably answer differently. The question becomes much more difficult when we consider the five other more weighty minor characters.

The Mayor seems to be the perfect example of the male petit bourgeois politician, fanatically proud of his little undistinguished town and prepared to over-varnish its cultural assets: 'Goethe hat hier übernachtet, Brahms ein Quartett komponiert. Diese Werte verpflichten' (p.89/p.69). The Mayor it is too who has to welcome Claire Zachanassian as the possible saviour of a town which has gone to the dogs. At the beginning he is more than willing to use Alfred Ill — already designated as his successor in office — and his earlier connection to Claire to get hold of her millions. This leads to one of the great comic set-pieces of the play: the Mayor's speech at the banquet (pp.49-51/pp.42-44). Having garnered information on Claire from Alfred and the Teacher, he unwittingly, and sometimes wittingly, turns Claire's less than respectable youthful escapades into glowing bourgeois virtues. Her stoning of the police when a criminal was led away becomes 'Gerechtigkeitsliebe' (although the stoning must not be mentioned), her stealing of potatoes for an old widow in order to be able to sleep with Ill in a bed instead of in the woods or in the barn, becomes her 'Sinn für Wohltätigkeit', and her school record, miserable but for 'Pflanzen- und Tierkunde', is praised as a model and a sign of her sympathy for those who are in need.

To be fair to the Mayor, he initially knows nothing of Alfred's seduction and desertion of Claire, which makes his proclaimed disgust when it is revealed in Act II at least understandable, if not excusable: 'Für den Posten eines Bürgermeisters sind gewisse Forderungen sittlicher Natur zu stellen, die Sie nicht mehr erfüllen, das müssen Sie einsehen,' he tells Alfred (p.91/pp.70-71), nevertheless with the others he goes ahead ordering new luxuries. Yet it was the Mayor who had fiercely told Claire when she announced her demand that Alfred be killed:

Noch sind wir in Europa, noch sind wir keine Heiden.
Ich lehne im Namen der Stadt Güllen das Angebot ab.

> Im Namen der Menschlichkeit. Lieber bleiben wir arm
> denn blutbefleckt.   (p.59/p.50)

And it is the Mayor who drives Alfred into the murder trap at the end
and then pronounces the hypocritical 'Tod aus Freude' (p.177/p.130).

Sexual mores too have changed since 1956, hence it is possible
that Alfred's seduction and desertion of Claire had so disgusted the
Mayor and his Christian principles that he felt entitled to sacrifice
his colleague and friend 'for the greater good'. The same dilemma
confronts the Clergyman.[5] He too has seen his church and its
possessions sold off to pay the town's debts, but he too tries to hang
on to his old principles and beliefs. When the Mayor suggests that
Claire is the town's only hope of survival, the Clergyman mutters:
'Außer Gott', but is harshly told: 'Aber der zahlt nicht' (p.11/p.18),
and he is shocked when Claire warns him that they might have to
reintroduce the death penalty in Güllen (pp.27-29/p.29). In his major
scene with Ill, we see that he too, like the Mayor, is prepared to
forget these Christian principles, particularly one — that all life is
sacred — in order that the town may survive (pp.97-101/pp.73-76).
He tries to assure the terrified shopkeeper that his fears are
unnecessary, that only Alfred's bad conscience has provoked them:
'Die Hölle liegt in Ihnen [...]. Der Grund unserer Furcht liegt in
unserem Herzen, liegt in unserer Sünde' (p.99/p.74).

But Alfred has seen the Clergyman's gun, ostensibly there to
kill Claire's escaped black panther, and believes that the Clergyman
is out to kill him too. The church's newly-acquired bell does little to
convince him otherwise, but only at the end of the conversation does
the Clergyman reveal his true feelings when he admits that all are
weak, Christians and heathens alike, and he begs Alfred to flee to
save them all from the temptation of killing him for the money.
When we notice that the Clergyman's last appearance is shortly

---

[5]This is possibly the best translation of 'Der Pfarrer' here, since we are told
in the *Randnotizen, alphabetisch geordnet* (in the programme of the Zürich
premiere in 1962) that there are '52 Prozent Protestanten, 45 Prozent
Katholiken, 3 Prozent sonstige' in Güllen. (These notes are now in WA5,
pp.137-41, but unfortunately not in the Routledge edition.)

before Alfred is led to his death, and that he there offers to pray for Alfred, albeit helplessly, and then retires into the crowd as if he would wash his hands of the whole affair, we just wonder if Dürrenmatt's early Calvinist upbringing with his clergyman father made him baulk at involving the Clergyman more directly in the murder. Or does he perhaps stand for the kind of decency which tries to remain uninvolved? Either way, Dürrenmatt's attacks on established religion grew sharper in his later works.

These five minor characters being examined represent, of course, the Establishment of Dürrenmatt's own society: politics, the Church, education, medicine and the Law, and it is this society which he places in the dock and which gives this play its particular significance.

Education has long been the cornerstone of German(ic) society; the teacher or the professor has always been both the model and the vilified antagonist for its members. Many a man or woman in Germanic society who has not made much of life will blame it on his or her teacher: 'Der/Die hat mich nie gemocht'. The reason is that, unlike in the British system where school examinations are validated by objective outside bodies, the Germanic teacher has a personal involvement in his or her candidate's final assessment. German literature abounds in stories and plays about vindictive, even cruel, professors and teachers. We have already noted how Frank Wedekind's *Frühlings Erwachen* was a savage indictment of the old German education system (see above, p.30); Heinrich Mann's *Novelle* of 1905, *Professor Unrat*, tells a similar tale, this time of a pedantic teacher who goes off the rails and takes up with a common cabaret singer who then degrades him to the position of a clown in a cabaret act. It was made into the famous 1930 film *Der blaue Engel* with Emil Jannings and Marlene Dietrich.

There is no such sexual delinquency in Dürrenmatt's portrayal of his Teacher, but his righteous claim to moral superiority is stressed in his very first remarks to Claire on her arrival at the station when, in his best pedantic *Hochdeutsch*, he asks 'als Rektor des Güllener Gymnasiums und Liebhaber der edlen Frau Musica sei es mir erlaubt, mit einem schlichten Volkslied aufzuwarten', and Claire brings him down with her unpedantic and colloquial: 'Schießen Sie los, Lehrer, mit Ihrem schlichten Volkslied', which is then comically and contemptuously lost in the noise of an oncoming train (p.25/pp.27-28). Dürrenmatt continues to represent him as a man whose values are those of a past and lost age, particularly the age of Greece and Rome which played such a major role in the curricula of Germanic grammar schools, values which Dürrenmatt has never ceased to attack when they were misused, as having foisted on to our age ideas and ideals literally foreign to it: 'Dulce et decorum est pro patria mori', for example — Horace's 'it is beautiful and honourable to die for one's country', the belief in war for aggrandizement, in strong leaders, in power politics and so on. The Teacher is, however, the only one in the group who senses the inhumanity of Claire which might well bode ill: 'Kommt mir vor,' he says, ' wie eine Parze, wie eine griechische Schicksalsgöttin,' like Clotho indeed, one of the three avenging Furies who spun the thread of human life and therefore had control over our destinies (p.35/p.34).

Although the Teacher takes his part too in the frightening scene at the end of Act II when Ill makes to leave the town but cannot (pp.106-09/pp.80-85), Dürrenmatt makes a more worthy character out of him in Act III, firstly when he attempts to persuade Claire to drop her demand for revenge: '...helfen Sie armen, schwachen, aber rechtschaffenen Leuten, ein etwas würdigeres Leben zu führen, ringen Sie sich zur reinen Menschlichkeit durch!' (p.119/pp.90-91), only to be rejected on the grounds that humanity is only a matter for rich financiers; and then, when in despair he takes to drink, climbs on to a beer barrel and harangues his fellow-Güllener only to be rejected again, not just by them but also by Ill himself, who is determined to accept his fate, he says: 'Ich wollte Ihnen helfen. Aber man schlug mich nieder und auch Sie wollten es nicht' (p.135/p.102). In a touching speech, he admits how he too will forget all his cherished principles: 'Auch ich werde mitmachen,' but not before he prophesies grimly, 'daß auch zu uns einmal eine alte Dame kommen wird', (pp.137-39/p.103); and here Dürrenmatt was clearly pointing the figure at others, people and countries, to whom one day a similar Nemesis will come. It is a powerful speech and makes the Teacher — curiously, and only here — Dürrenmatt's mouthpiece; in the last act, however, when the Mayor calls on the Teacher to speak to the assembly, we hear the voice of the broken man who must 'mitmachen'. His plea for justice ('Gerechtigkeit') is of course ambiguous, since he knows full well, and better than most, that two wrongs cannot make a right. What Ill did to Claire was indeed an injustice, but what the Güllener are going to do to Ill is at least as great an injustice; moreover, it is going to be rewarded with luxury. His plea, not to forget the virtues and values of their past, 'die den Wert unseres Abendlands ausmachen', is linked to his plea that the Güllener should only accept Claire's money 'wenn ihr unter keinen Umständen in einer Welt der Ungerechtigkeit mehr leben könnt', and as we know that they have decided to ignore that plea and murder Ill for the money, the tragicomic potential of the speech is obvious (pp.165-67/pp.121-22).

Timo Tiusanen suggests that the speech really has three layers: the reporter sees it as 'social criticism', the Güllener as a condemnation of Ill's crime, while the Teacher is despairingly trying to show the Güllener the error of their ways. Whether the Teacher's despairing cry is like that of the intellectuals in Hitler's Germany is more debatable (*76*, pp.238-39).

The Policeman's role is weightier than the Doctor's; although Dürrenmatt was writing his play before the late 1960s when the traditional processes of law in most European countries began to be questioned and the police forces were to be attacked as repressive, sometimes brutal arms of the Establishment, no German-speaking audience could forget how a German state police force had once behaved.

The Policeman greets Claire with more aplomb than the others and seems much more self-possessed, even joking with this weird arrival: he is asked whether he turns a blind eye now and then. 'Das schon, gnädige Frau. Wo käme ich in Güllen sonst hin?' — implying that Güllen society is perhaps not as respectable as the welcoming party would suggest (p.27/p.28). One has the feeling that he is the archetypal Western sheriff in an American hick town in the pocket of the Mayor and his cronies. This is suggested too by his confidential reports on Claire and Alfred's conversations in the Peterschen Scheune which he seemed to have witnessed or overheard (p.35/p.34). He is clearly much more than just a policeman; this is underlined when Ill visits him in the course of his visits to the Mayor, the Teacher and the Clergyman.

When Ill appears, we have, at first sight, a picture of a true village policeman, with slow, deliberate speech, drinking his beer and lighting his pipe. To Ill's fevered demand that Claire Zachanassian be arrested, the Policeman answers with deliberate officialese that Ill must first report the lady. 'Ob sie dann verhaftet wird, entscheidet die Polizei' (p.77/p.61). Then, in a comic scene of illogicality, he tries to prove to Ill that Claire's demand that he be killed can only be taken as a joke. 'Für so was bietet man tausend oder vielleicht zweitausend, mehr bestimmt nicht' (p.79/p.62). And if the suggestion were a serious one, then the lady could not be taken seriously, for she must then be mad. In addition, Ill cannot be threatened by a suggestion, only by the carrying out of a suggestion. Even when Ill tells him that the villagers are all buying expensive goods — and new yellow shoes — the Policeman reminds him that he is lucky, that his business is booming, and that he too is wearing new yellow shoes. This impressive dramatic scene ends when the Policeman, now a much less naive village bobby, a new gold tooth shining in his mouth, loads his gun, pointing it at Ill, and claims that he is off to find Claire's black panther. Ill can only groan: 'Mich jagt ihr, mich' (p.85/p.66).

It is a fine and typical Dürrenmattian scene, laden with paradox and irony. The defender of the peace is himself a hypocritical 'Mitmacher' who, while assuring Ill ('Die Polizei ist da, den Gesetzen Respekt zu verschaffen, für Ordnung zu sorgen, den Bürger zu schützen') is obviously hand in glove with those preparing for Ill's murder (p.85/p.65). His true colours are shown at the very end, when, while the others go through with the charade of an 'honourable' *exitus* carried off with bourgeois gentility, he pulls Alfred to his feet with a 'Steh auf, du Schwein', and has to be chastised by the Mayor (p.177/p.129).

Finally the Doctor. His role is a very minor one, yet it is he who has to pronounce the biggest lie of all: that Alfred died of a heart attack. In his very first appearance, Claire asks him if he ever makes out death certificates and if so, then in future to certify 'Herzchlag' (p.45/p.30). The 1980 version omits the rather unflattering description of his person: a fifty-year-old, slightly-built man with a moustache, bristling black hair and, ominously, 'Schmisse im Gesicht'; the reference is to the scars 'earned' by German students in fencing duels in the old days of the *Studentenverbindungen*; again then, a relic of the traditional Establishment. We see him accompanying the Teacher to meet Claire in the barn at the beginning of Act III, but he contributes only a few words to the discussion and, at the end, has to ask the Teacher: 'Mein Gott, was sollen wir tun?' The answer, 'Was uns das Gewissen vorschreibt, Doktor Nüßlin', raises the Teacher in our estimation, as it lowers the Doctor who had obviously never considered that option and may therefore have no conscience at all, we may think (p.119/p.91).

The remainder of the characters listed under 'Die Besuchten' in the *Personenliste* are in fact the other characters from the village, 'Menschen wie wir alle', as Dürrenmatt wrote in the *Anmerkung*.

> Sie sind nicht böse zu zeichnen, durchaus nicht; zuerst entschlossen, das Angebot abzulehnen, machen sie nun Schulden, doch nicht im Vorsatz, Ill zu töten, sondern aus Leichtsinn, aus einem Gefühl heraus, es lasse sich alles schon arrangieren.   (p.189/p.143)

This, the author suggests, is how Act II should be played. Modern performances that I have seen tended to stress the evil that lies within us all and to make the villagers' purchases seem much less innocent, but that indication should only emerge after Ill has noted, in Act II, that Helmesberger (Der Zweite) is wearing new yellow shoes (p.75/pp.59-60), and that the others, Der Erste (Hofbauer) and the two women, defend their purchases with: 'Man kann doch nicht ewig in den alten Schuhen herumlaufen,' which then brings forth Ill's

anguished, tragic and most dramatic cry: 'Womit wollt ihr zahlen?
Womit wollt ihr zahlen? Womit? Womit?' — a perfect example of
Dürrenmatt's paradoxical method of creating tragedy out of comedy
(p.75/p.60).

Otherwise the four Bürger are used as a type of Greek chorus,
summing up the villagers' economic tribulations in Act I, the doings
of Claire and her retinue in Act II and, as part of the *Gemeinde* in
Act III, driving Ill to his death. The author's most interesting
innovation in the play is that classic speech form which he gives to
these four and which I noted as *stichomythia* (cf. footnote 1 on p.14):

> Der Maler: Der D-Zug!
> Der Erste: Hält!
> Der Zweite: In Güllen!
> Der Dritte: Im verarmtesten —
> Der Vierte: lausigsten —
> Der Erste: erbärmlichsten Nest der Strecke
> Venedig-Stockholm! (p.15/p.21)

The effect on the stage is to heighten the comic effect and, at the
same time, the dramatic impact, since the single statement is
multiplied by six, as it were.

So these may be minor characters but they are an essential part
of the plot, moving it forward, as we shall see, and providing most of
the comedy by their wooden (in the forest, literally!) responses. A
good director would ensure that the roles, especially of Der Erste and
Der Zweite, were played by competent actors. The others of the
'Besuchten' group really only have one-liners to speak.

We turn now to the Besucher, Claire's grotesque retinue, who
bring that 'Frösteln' into the play of which the nineteenth-century
German dramatist Friedrich Hebbel wrote in his definition of
tragicomedy:

> Man mögte [=möchte] vor Grausen erstarren, doch die
> Lachmuskeln zucken sogleich; man mögte sich durch ein
> Gelächter von dem ganzen unheimlichen Eindruck

befreien, doch ein Frösteln beschleicht uns wieder, ehe
es uns das gelingt. (*40*, p.379)

The stage direction tells us how the strange company should look.
Firstly, the Butler (Boby): about eighty, with black glasses (often a
sign of malevolence in films and television); Gatte VII (Moby): tall,
slim, with a black moustache and his fishing tackle; then later the
two Herculean, gum-chewing monsters with the sedan chair (Roby
and Toby), Sing-Sing gangsters released from the electric chair; and
finally, the two eunuchs, Koby and Loby. They are all to play
important parts in the development of the plot: the Butler, the former
high court judge in Güllen (and named as Hofer, from 'Hof', meaning
'court'), now hired by Claire as a butler to enable her to remind
Alfred of the legal paternity case against him; then the two eunuchs,
Alfred's former witnesses, Jakob Hühnlein ('Hühnlein' meaning 'little
chicken'), and Ludwig Sparr ('Sparr' suggesting a little madness),
who swore in 1910 that they had slept with Claire (or Klara) and
made her pregnant. Claire's two monsters had flushed them out of
their emigration in Canada and Australia respectively, castrated and
blinded them and then returned them to Güllen to retract their
statements, and they allow Claire to demand the justice that she can
now afford: 'Gerechtigkeit für eine Milliarde' (p.59/p.49).

It is perhaps instructive at this point to recall the reasons for
the rhyming '-oby' names. Claire says that Gatte VII is really called
Pedro, but that she calls him Moby: 'Es paßt auch besser zu Boby,
wie der Kammerdiener heißt. Den hat man schließlich fürs Leben, da
müssen sich dann eben die Gatten nach seinem Namen richten'
(p.23/p.26); and we recall that Gatte VIII will be called Hoby and
Gatte IX Zoby. The whole process intensifies the other-worldliness
of Claire and shows her contempt for the sex who so degraded her:
she reduces them to mere numbers.

Die Sonstigen and Die Lästigen present a world used to the
normal turn of events, now disoriented and alienated by the
cataclysmic happenings in Güllen. The Kondukteur represents the
smooth-running (probably Swiss), efficient railway company, the
trains of which all bear the functional names (cf. pp.30-31 above)

which illustrate the yawning gap between the economic wealth of the rest of the country and Güllen: the Gudrun (a name from the famous Germanic mediaeval sagas popularized by Richard Wagner's operas); the Rasende Roland (probably from Ariosto's 1516 play *Roland furieux*); the Diplomat (from the world of international politics); the Loreley (the name of the legendary rock on the Rhine) and the Börsianer (redolent of Zürich gnomes); and none of these stop in the depressed little town which bears the name of the Swiss liquid manure which we first encountered in *Mondfinsternis*, and which has now witnessed the arrival of a woman who makes such trains stop.

Just as the Zugführer's role is to allow us to see Claire break straightaway with convention by stopping that Rasenden Roland train, so the pressmen (nowadays the 'paparazzi') show us the arrogance and the insincerity of the big-town media come to cover an event in a little town which for them could not possibly have any sinister undertones. They are willing to believe, for the sake of a good story, that Alfred and Claire, youthful friends, went out together until Alfred met Mathilde ('die Leidenschaft', p.127/p.97) and married her, while Claire renounced Alfred 'auf ihre stille, edle Art'. And now she has returned at Alfred's behest to share her good fortune with the town of her youth. The two major scenes for them (Act III, pp.125-33/pp.95-101) and the parodistic assembly (Act III, pp.161-79/pp.118-31) present a richly comic picture of the intrusion of the media into modern life. Each of the Mayor's phrases, swallowed whole by the reporters, are deeply ambiguous and allow that 'Frösteln', of which Hebbel wrote (see above, p.41) to creep over the audience when the innocent reporter interprets them in his naive way. Even more effective is the radio reporter's misunderstanding of the Teacher's agonized plea for justice; we, the audience, know that his cry: 'es geht darum, ob wir Gerechtigkeit verwirklichen wollen' is already ambiguous; but when the reporter discerns in the speech 'eine sittliche Größe, wie wir sie heute — leider — nicht mehr allzuoft finden', the author has woven a marvellously tragicomic pattern which also contains a frightening denunciation of the greed and corruption in modern western society. As Karl S. Guthke wrote:

'Die Tragikomödie taucht aber jeweils dort auf, wo eine geltende Sicherheit ihre Verbindlichkeit verliert, fragwürdig wird' (*37*, p.25). Güllen represents this 'secure tradition' which Dürrenmatt never ceases to attack.

4. Der Besuch der alten Dame: *The Major Characters and the Dramatic Structure*

In Dürrenmatt's radio play (*Hörspiel*) *Abendstunde im Spätherbst* (1956), the main character, a distinguished author, one of Dürrenmatt's many self-portraits, Maximilian Friedrich Korbes, groans to an inquisitive visitor: 'Ich wurde schon tiefenpsychologisch, katholisch, protestantisch, existentialistisch, buddhistisch und marxistisch gedeutet' (WA9, p.169-96), and one feels that this has been the fate of *Der Besuch der alten Dame* too, subjected to every possible interpretation, which on the other hand perhaps explains its firm position in the list of post-war European classics. E.S. Dick, for example, stressed the symbolic elements in the work (26); J.C. Hortenbach wrote that '*Der Besuch der alten Dame* is a modern presentation of the Passion Play, not only in part or in grotesque or nihilistic distortion, but in the full sense of the word' (46, p.147), while M. Peppard agreed with me that 'there is no single, simple message or moral in *The Visit*, but rather a powerful action with a wide range of suggestibility' (65, p.62). Dick's theory, which treats the play as the 'Ritualspiel der Tötung des Sündenbocks', which in turn leads to the regeneration of the town, enjoyed popularity at a time of social unrest in Germany and on the Continent.

I have written more than once of the presence of ambiguity, of paradox, in this or that scene of the play; this is the essence of Dürrenmattian drama. Again and again, he stresses that it is this ambiguity, what he calls the 'Doppelbödigkeit' of the action, which makes the drama dramatic, and it is this rich ambiguity which makes *Der Besuch der alten Dame* such a fascinating play for actors and audiences.

Having examined the minor roles in the play, it is time now to turn to the two main characters, Alfred and Claire, and to consider how Dürrenmatt has structured his drama around them. My examination of the story *Mondfinsternis* showed where the 'Einfall' for the play came from: the basic idea of a man returning to his home village after years in emigration, bent on exacting revenge for an injustice done in his youth. I found however (see above, p.26) that Walt Lotcher's revenge was hardly calculated, indeed that he was not quite sure on whom the revenge should fall, nor indeed why it should fall at all. He admitted that it was not anger that had made him want Mani Döufu dead but a simple longing to relive that part of his youth now that he was fairly sure, after several heart attacks, that he would not live much longer. How far removed this is from Claire's carefully-planned, white-hot desire to gain the ultimate sacrifice for her dishonour. (It might however just be noticed in passing that there is never any question of Kläri Zurbriggen having felt dishonoured in the story. The author takes there a very male view of the situation.)

The audience knows from the programme details that the play is taking place in the 'Kleinstadt' Güllen, and if they know some Southwest or Swiss German, they might well wonder, as they take their seats, why the author has given the town such a name. Duden's *Deutsches Universalwörterbuch* (1989) gives under *Gülle* 'flüssiger Stalldünger, der sich aus Jauche, Kot und Wasser zusammensetzt' i.e. liquid dung or manure. The audience would have suspected some particular motive here, but it was not until *Mondfinsternis* was published that we realized that Dürrenmatt had found the perfect symbol for the stinking hypocrisy of his imaginary village in the name 'Güllen'.[6]

---

[6] In the *Randnotizen* we read under *Güllen*: 'Name einer Stadt zwischen Kaffigen und Kalberstadt [...]. Der Name der Stadt soll auf Begehren der stimmfähigen Bürger in Gülden umgewandelt werden' (WA5, pp.138-39). N.B. 'Ein Kaff' is 'eine kleine langweilige Ortschaft', while 'Kalberstadt' is a 'town of calves'.

Act I

The opening scene of Act I presents a picture of complete economic desolation. Dürrenmatt's stage directions are very important for directors, actors and readers alike since, as we shall see in the opening of *Die Physiker* also, they often take the form of *explications de texte*. Here the ruined station with the sign 'GÜLLEN' and the equally ruined town 'angedeutet' in the background, the 'kleine Häuschen' (of which we are to learn more shortly) also falling apart; and five men, four on a seat and the fifth 'aufs unbeschreiblichste verwahrlost', holding up a poster with the words 'WILLKOMMEN KLÄRI', prepare us for the presence of the welcoming party and the eventual arrival of the 'old lady'.

From the five men we have a type of classical exposition, relating the sorrows of Güllen, the closing down of the Bockmann- and Wagner-Werke and the Platz-an-der-Sonne-Hütte and the consequent need to live on the dole. We also have from them the first news of the 'Milliardärin' who has already begun to help neighbouring towns in similar distress; economic ruin has evidently hit the whole region. Trains keep rushing past to make us realize how insignificant Güllen has become; according to these locals, it was once a cultural centre:

> Der Vierte: Goethe hat hier übernachtet. Im Gasthof zum
> Goldenen Apostel.
> Der Dritte: Brahms ein Quartett komponiert. (p.5/pp.14-15),

empty phrases here but which will be repeated later by the Mayor to Alfred with more sinister significance (cf. p.89/p.69).

This cultural charade continues when the welcoming party arrives, led by the pompous Mayor. They are all shabbily dressed, and among them is Alfred Ill, almost sixty-five years old, we are told. No good explanation has been given or found for the name 'Ill'. It was clearly never meant to relate to the English word 'ill'. The best proposal was put forward by Kurt Fickert (in *33*): that it relates to the French 'il' in the sense of 'everyman'. The very free translation of the play by Maurice Valency in 1958 turned 'Ill' into 'Anton Schill' (which is an Austrian surname, incidentally). But worse was to come: Ben Barzman's screenplay for the 1964 film made by 20th Century Fox had 'Ill' (played by Anthony Quinn) become 'Serge Miller'. Fortunately, Claire Zachanassian (played by Ingrid Bergman) retained her original name. Patrick Bowles's is the best translation (see *14*).

The party is expecting the billionairess to arrive by the normal local train, the 1.13 from the neighbouring town of Kalberstadt, which will stop in Güllen; the overall sense of desolation increases when the bailiff (depressingly named Glutz) emerges from the public toilet to inform them all that he has come to impound the whole town, which moves the Mayor to remind Ill that everything depends on him and his old friendship with this rich old lady, now named Claire Zachanassian, but formerly simply Kläri Wäscher. Zachanassian is one of Dürrenmatt's 'erfundenen Namen'. In the *Randnotizen* (under Zachanassian) we read: 'Claire, geborene Wäscher, 1892 [...]. Name zusammengezogen aus Zacharoff, Onassis, Gulbenkian (letzterer beerdigt in Zürich). Wohltätige Dame' (p.141). All three men were enormously rich and connected (usually by account numbers) with Switzerland in one way or another. 'Kläri' (meaning clear or clean) and 'Wäscher' (meaning the 'washer') are also symbolic and functional names. Alfred has soiled something supposedly pure, although Claire's account of her youthful escapades makes this a little doubtful.

From the beginning, Alfred cleverly conceals any suggestion of improper behaviour between Kläri and himself and presents themselves as impetuous young lovers, giving the Mayor a favourable picture of a pretty young girl eager to help others. The unprecedented stopping of the 11.27 express from Venice to Stockholm, the Rasende Roland, brings consternation, and the significant remark from the overwhelmed Stationmaster: 'Die Naturgesetze sind aufgehoben' (p.15/p.21). Thus Claire is already suggested as being other-worldly, beyond the natural laws of our earth, and her first appearance underlines this feeling: the stage direction, as usual very precise, tells us that she is sixty-three (the

1980 version has her as sixty-two), red-haired, wearing a pearl necklace, huge gold rings on her arm and 'dressed to kill' ('aufgedonnert'), but on the other hand a lady of the *grand monde*, with a strange charm despite all this grotesqueness. It is a very important description, especially for young directors, who continually make Claire into an eighty-year-old woman, seemingly believing that there is little difference between the ages of sixty-two or three and eighty (p.17/pp.21-22).

Claire's first words obviously caused Dürrenmatt some difficulty. The Routledge edition, based on the 1957 (original) Arche edition, has: 'Ist hier Güllen?' This now becomes 'Bin ich in Güllen?' (p.17/p.22) — perhaps a more personal remark, nearly filled with longing but also with contempt, both for the condition of the town and the bourgeois pedantry of the Swiss-like guard ('Die Pünktlichkeit des Fahrplans ist oberstes Prinzip') and, of course, by analogy, contempt for Switzerland's own pedantic mores. Her own brusque colloquial language with the guard also helps us to place her character: 'Sie sind ein Schafskopf', she tells him determinedly, 'Sie wollen mir wohl zumuten, eine halbe Stunde durch diese Gegend zu dampfen' (pp.17, 19/p.23), and finally: 'Brausen Sie mit Ihrem Zug davon' ('Buzz off with your train') — all this compared to the stiff *Hochdeutsch* of the guard, but also of the opening speech of the Mayor, whose pomposity is pricked when the speech is lost in the noise of the departing train. Thus a 1956 Zürich audience was already on the defensive.

The first meeting of our two main characters (pp.21-23/pp.25-26) is revealing. Alfred misunderstands Claire's ironic remark: 'Es war wunderbar, all die Tage, da wir zusammen waren', as meaning that she has come back just to see him. So he turns to the Teacher with: 'Sehen Sie, Herr Lehrer, *die* habe ich im Sack', and her disparaging remarks about his figure ('fett', 'grau und versoffen') bring from him the flattering but clearly insincere: 'Doch *du* bist die gleiche geblieben, Zauberhexchen.' Claire's derisive reply and her pointing to her artificial left leg, the result of a car accident, might give us a clue to subsequent events, for she speaks in the same sarcastic, derogatory tone to the Teacher, the Policeman and the

Clergyman, particularly when she suggests that Güllen might reintroduce the death penalty (pp.27-29/p.29). Finally, the Mayor is put down when Claire insists on being taken to the town in her sedan chair. The town sees the Herculean Roby and Toby for the first time, the two gangsters released from Sing-Sing at Claire's behest, while we learn that the chair is a present from the French president. The audience laughs at the fantasy, but is there not a faint prickling of the hairs at the back of our necks? This is clearly now no ordinary, sixty-three-year-old but someone extraordinary, someone who is above the laws of this world and who can direct dignitaries, governments — and fate — as she will.

When the action moves to the Goldenen Apostel, the main hotel in Güllen ('where Goethe stayed'), Dürrenmatt indulges once again in comic, yet eery symbolism: the very name of the hotel, its gilded apostolic emblem swaying in the middle of the room; the many references, now and later, to 'golden' or 'yellow'; and, not least, the biblical reference probably uppermost in Dürrenmatt's mind: 'Therefore all things whatsoever ye would that men should do to you, do ye even so to them' (Matthew 7. 12) which broods over the whole action. The stage direction for the hotel scene tells us: 'Alles verschlissen, verstaubt, zerbrochen, verstunken, vermodert', a godsend for a modern stage designer. It is in this ambience that the Mayor, the Teacher and the Clergyman, later to be joined by the Policeman, discuss their hopes based on Ill's past relationship with this strange woman, with her many cases, her black panther in its cage, and her coffin, all of which the Mayor excuses with the comic remark: 'Weltberühmte Damen haben ihre Marotten' (p.33/p.33). (The Clergyman has this line in the 1980 version.)

We move now to the first important meeting between Klara and Alfred in their Konradsweilerwald, and the tragicomic scene set by the four men (Der Erste etc.) acting in marionette-fashion the parts of trees, as children used to do in Christmas pantomimes of times past, but here the humour has an underlying eeriness: these too are surreal elements. And it is in this symbolic setting that we hear how Alfred, then nineteen or so, and Claire, then seventeen, made love under the beech (a theme from *Mondfinsternis* perhaps?) more than forty-five years ago; how Alfred then married Mathilde, and Claire, who had become a Hamburg prostitute, married the Armenian billionaire, Zachanassian; and how Alfred, 'ein verkrachter Krämer in einem verkrachten Städtchen' (p.39/p.38), is now ruined and living in hellish poverty with his family, while Claire is not only rich but — and we shudder as we hear her say: 'Und ich bin die Hölle geworden' — we sense that this woman is not of this world. Claire retains the upper hand too as Alfred begins to beg for money to restore Güllen and receives from Claire the promise: 'Ich lasse das Städtchen meiner Jugend nicht im Stich' (p.41/p.38), but a close examination of Claire's answers makes us realize that they too are all ambiguous, all 'doppelbödig'. She knows Alfred's weak character and plays upon her knowledge that he thinks that she has just returned to relive old times with him.

The end of the scene re-emphasizes Claire's other-worldliness when Ill discovers that practically all her limbs are artificial — the result of car and aeroplane accidents in exotic places, but the main point for the plot is that Claire is immortal: '[...] bin nicht umzubringen' (p.43/p.40). Now we are certain that she is not as other people.

The banquet in Act I is, of course, the scene which precipitates the main action of the play and to which all the deeply ambiguous previous action has been leading. It is prefaced by more of Claire's strange remarks: she asks the gymnast if he has ever strangled anyone, which makes the Doctor shudder: 'Solche Späße gehen durch Mark und Bein' (p.47/p.41), but Ill finds it screamingly funny, although he is fated to remember them at the end of the play when the gymnast waits for him in the 'Gasse' (p.175/p.128). The banquet then begins with the Mayor's comically inaccurate speech when he misinterprets Alfred's and the Teacher's reports on Claire by attempting to present what were clearly her youthful misdeeds as social virtues. Claire's chilling answer, that most of the Mayor's congratulatory remarks were ill-founded and that she has few claims to social virtues, ends with her offer to give each family 500 million with another 500 million to the town, in total, a sum of one billion. The 1980 version alters 'verteilt auf jede Familie' to 'verteilt auf alle

Familien' which seems to alter the sense slightly. It will be recalled that Walt Lotcher in *Mondfinsternis* would give each of the fourteen families 'eine Million'. However, the Mayor in the later version still stutters: 'Eine Milliarde'.

Now come the conditions: firstly, that Claire, with this billion, will buy herself justice, but, more directly, 'eine Milliarde für Güllen, wenn jemand Alfred Ill tötet' (p.57/p.49). This last and final condition is made, however, only after Claire has produced that damning evidence from the past: the judge, now her butler, and the two blinded eunuchs whom Alfred had bribed, so that he might be able to deny the paternity of Claire's baby which only lived for a year, after Claire had become a prostitute. Ill becomes progressively worried and exasperated until his protestation that all is in the past and 'das Leben ging doch längst weiter!' (p.59/p.49) is answered by Claire's cold remark that she is now what he made her and that she has forgotten nothing of the past. She has now 'removed the distance of the years', as Alfred had playfully asked her to do when they were in the wood, and now she wants justice for what she has suffered during these intervening years.

Act I closes with the Mayor's agonized, pompous and now famous defiance: 'Noch sind wir in Europa, noch sind wir keine Heiden. Ich lehne im Namen der Stadt Güllen das Angebot ab. Im Namen der Menschlichkeit. Lieber bleiben wir arm denn blutbefleckt' (p.59/p.50). But somehow that little word 'denn' instead of the more modern 'als' makes us feel that his and the townspeople's later behaviour will be somewhat different from these noble words. Like Claire, the audience 'waits'.

Act II

The act begins in Alfred's shop in front of the hotel with its balcony visible. The audience sees Roby and Toby ominously carrying wreaths into the Goldenen Apostel while Alfred's daughter scrubs the floor of the shop and the son smokes a cigarette. We are lulled by the seeming normality; Alfred is sure that, despite the wreaths (for the coffin that Claire has brought with her), the town is still behind him as it was at the banquet; his children also seem to be acting normally, the girl is off to the labour exchange to look for a job, the boy is off to the station to do likewise. Alfred is proud of them: 'Gute Kinder, brave Kinder' (p.63/p.52).

The facade of normality crumbles when, firstly, a voice is heard from the balcony: 'Reich mir mein linkes Bein herüber, Boby', and the audience is reminded of the inhuman visitor; secondly, there begins a stream of visits from the townsfolk to Alfred's store to buy the sort of goods that they could never afford before: cigarettes, milk, butter, bread, chocolate, schnaps, cognac and tobacco, but all of the better brands; they all also ask Alfred to put them on account: 'Schreiben's auf' (p.63/p.55). At first, Alfred has no worries, 'weil wir zusammenhalten müssen' (p.63/p.53), but as the scene progresses, doubts arise in his mind.

Meanwhile the second strand of the plot is developing when Claire appears on the balcony with her new husband, Gatte VIII (Hoby) and interjects comments accompanied by the intermittent strains of guitar chords from Roby, one of the 'monsters'. These both fill in her background and prepare us for what is about to happen. Her remark as she appears on the balcony: 'Ich bin wieder montiert' (p.65/p.54), and her position high above the action, on the hotel balcony, place her symbolically as an other-worldly phenomenon in another world, looking down on the poor denizens of Güllen.

Although the new husband is at first delighted with his new home, and only later is made to show how unaware he is of the true situation by his ambiguous dismissal of Güllen's Swiss-like peaceful complacency, he senses 'sorgloser Friede', 'Gemütlichkeit' and then 'Keine Größe, keine Tragik'. Even this tiny role contributes a little to the feeling of inevitable tragedy (p.95/p.73). Claire (his 'Hopsi') shows again however that this husband too is only a substitute for the Alfred that she could not have, and her interest in him is marginal and comic: 'Setz dich, Hoby, rede nicht. Die Landschaft seh ich selber, und Gedanken sind nicht deine Stärke' (p.73/p.58). She will soon be rid of him too. Claire's husbands have covered a wide range of types and professions and add to the impression that she is a 'Frau Welt', not bound to time or space: Gatte I was

Zachanassian (in oil); Gatte II owned Western Railways; Gatte III was Graf Holk, the Foreign Minister; Gatte IV was Lord Ismael, the Yorkshireman whom she seduced in Buckingham Palace; Gatte V was a surgeon; Gatte VI was a fashion designer who made all of her wedding dresses; Gatte VII, Moby, was in tobacco; Gatte VIII, Hoby, was a film star; and Gatte IX, Zoby, was a Nobel Prize winner.

Dürrenmatt cleverly keeps the two strands of the action physically apart, yet at the same time maintains the connection between them through odd remarks of the characters. The Güllener resent Claire's smoking expensive cigars, for example, while husband VIII only sees the romantic scene and a few housewives 'mit ihren kleinen Sorgen' (p.73/p.58); but it is the tragic development of these 'little worries' down below, which contrasts so strongly with the banalities exchanged between Claire and the husband above and which creates the dramatic tension of Act II.

Ill looks back on the reaction of the townspeople to Claire's offer at the banquet as the 'schönste Stunde' of his life, yet he gives a hostage to future fortune when he admits to Hofbauer that he knew that he had wronged Claire. It is from this point on — 'Ich bin ein alter Sünder, Hofbauer' (p.69/p.56) — that the Güllener turn against Alfred, while hypocritically assuring him that they will support him 'felsenfest' as the next mayor of the town (p.69/pp.56-57). When Alfred asks Helmesberger why he is wearing new, yellow shoes and then notices that all are wearing new, yellow shoes, the scales fall from his eyes and his thrice-repeated cry: 'Womit wollt ihr zahlen?' is intensely dramatic (p.75/p.60).[7]

It is at this point that the author introduces the black panther motif. We recall the Mayor's mention of Claire's panther in the cage (see above, p.50) and how it had been her nickname for Alfred (p.23/p.26); now it becomes a symbol of Alfred's isolation and

---

[7]Yellow is well known in colour symbolism, usually as a sign of deceit, cowardice or jealousy, and, on stage during this play, it is a remarkably clear indication for the audience of the hypocrisy of the Güllener, and their treachery. In addition there is a strong comic element in an 'assembly' of yellow shoes.

persecution: just as the panther escapes from the cage and is hunted by the guns of the leading citizens, so too is Alfred released from the regular confines of Güllen and, alone, is hunted down by these same citizens. One by one the Policeman (pp.77-85/pp.61-66), the Mayor (pp.87-95/pp.67-72) and the Clergyman (pp.95-101/pp.73-76) show him that, while assuring him of their support, they are ready to sacrifice him. Ill puts it most clearly to the Policeman when he explains how the town's debts will benefit the economy and how a strong economy will therefore lead to the need to kill him. Thus, all Claire needs to do is to sit on her balcony and wait, for 'ihr alle wartet' (p.83/p.65). But the Policeman assures him that that is all in his imagination.

When Alfred then meets the Mayor, we have the same mixture of hypocritical support and veiled threats: Alfred is told that he no longer has any moral right to demand Claire's arrest — the Mayor reminds him only too gladly of his crime — and there is now also no possibility of Alfred's becoming Mayor in succession to him; yet the Mayor still insists, as did the Policeman, that they have no intention of accepting Claire's offer, and that the wisest course is to forget the whole affair. But Ill has seen the Mayor's expensive cigar, his new silk tie, his yellow shoes, the new typewriter and finally the plan for the new Town Hall. It is the Mayor's defence of the latter which assures Ill (and the audience) that his fate is sealed, for the Mayor has insisted: 'wenn ich als Politiker nicht mehr das Recht hätte, an eine bessere Zukunft zu glauben, ohne gleich an ein Verbrechen denken zu müssen' then he would resign straightaway. 'Ihr habt mich schon zum Tode verurteilt,' cries Ill (pp.93-95/p.72).

The Clergyman is next to assure Alfred of his support. The scene reminds us that Dürrenmatt's father was a Calvinist clergyman himself and that the author was therefore familiar with church procedure. But this too is used for serio-comic effect: as Ill speaks of matters of life and death, the Clergyman is, ironically, preparing to be robed for a christening (p.99/p.75). His pious remarks are in part genuine: as a clergyman it is his duty to tell Ill that he has sinned and that he must repent; it is 'das Gespenst Ihres Gewissens' (p.97/p.74), he tells Ill, that pursues him. Ill should not therefore believe, just

because he has betrayed a young girl, that the town would betray
him. Yet here too Ill sees the signs of hypocrisy: the Church has just
acquired a new bell.

Thus we come to the second great set piece of the play: the
conclusion to Act II (pp.101-09/pp.80-85). We know that Ill is sure
that he is to be sacrificed. In the many commentaries on the play,
much has been made of the biblical nature of the theme (cf. *28, 45*
and *46*) and we see now that he has taken the Clergyman's final
panic-stricken cry to heart: 'Flieh, führe uns nicht in Versuchung,
indem du bleibst' (p.101/p.76), and has decided to leave the town.
The scene changes back to the station as in Act I, only this time we
see cranes in the background, indicating renovative work in
progress, and posters on the wall, indicating a new interest in
expensive holiday travel. Ill, a little suitcase in his hand, is met and
surrounded by the townspeople. It becomes a typical Dürrenmattian
scene, paradoxical and ambiguous, comic yet tragic. It seems at first
that the townspeople have come to prevent Ill from leaving the town.
Ill suggests that he is off to Kalberstadt and then 'nach Australien am
liebsten' (p.103/p.81), an idea which contrasts comically with the
'alten Köfferchen' in his hand; but first the Mayor, then the Teacher,
persuade him to stay. The Teacher says: 'Sie sehen ja, wie beliebt Sie
sind,' while the Policeman has already said (rather more ominously):
'Hier sind Sie am sichersten' (p.103/p.81); then suddenly, as the train
arrives, the mood changes dramatically and there is a chorus of:
'Eine gute Reise!' and 'Ein schönes, weiteres Leben!' (p.105/p.83)
which turns Ill into a hunted animal. He knows now why they have
all come: not to wish him goodbye — even if he has meant to leave
— but to ensure that he does not leave. The action becomes highly
charged as Ill accuses the crowd in a phrase reminiscent of the Bible:
'Einer wird mich zurückhalten' (p.107/p.83); one is reminded of
Jesus saying: 'Wahrlich ich sage euch: Einer unter euch wird mich
verraten' (Matthew 26. 21). As the crowd melts away, Ill, on his
knees, covers his face with his hands: 'Ich bin verloren!'
(p.109/p.85).

That final dramatic gesture tells us that Ill has accepted his
guilt and his punishment; Act III will show us the consequences. He

could have left the town, no one actually prevented him; but this is the first significant proof that he is beginning to prepare himself for Claire's revenge. He is the 'gedankenlose Mannsbild' of Dürrenmatt's *Anmerkung*, 'dem langsam etwas aufgeht, durch Furcht, durch Entsetzen, etwas höchst Persönliches' (p.189/p.143).

Act III

Having just witnessed Alfred Ill's surrender, the audience is ready for Claire's scene at the beginning of Act III. We are in the barn, the Peterschen Scheune, where Claire and Alfred used to meet to make love, and where Claire, now resplendent (and comically incongruous) in her bridal gown, sits in her sedan chair amidst decaying farm implements. This was where Claire and Alfred had their first reunion, as recalled by the Policeman, where according to him, they stood 'andächtig wie in einer Kirche' (p.35/P.34). It is therefore appropriate that Claire, after her wedding to (and immediate divorce from) her eighth (unsatisfactory) husband Hoby, should return to this scene of her first (and only) love.

One of Dürrenmatt's constant comic ploys is to bring down pompous characters; here, in the meeting between Claire, the Teacher and the Doctor, these are brought down by having to clamber over an old carriage to meet her. Although they are now both quite elegantly dressed, the dust from the carriage, their continual wiping away of sweat from their brows (partly caused by exertion, partly by their unease) and Claire's invitation to the Teacher to sit on a beer-barrel, puts them into a comically inferior position from the start. This is important, for they have come to plead, not for Alfred's life, as one might have expected, but that the billion that Claire has promised should be spent on restoring and/or developing the industries of Güllen. Only when Claire informs them that she has already bought up all the industrial works, the oil and the iron ore, does the Teacher — for the Doctor has little to say — beg her to forget her thirst for revenge: 'Ringen Sie sich zur reinen Menschlichkeit durch!' he cries. We have seen already how Dürrenmatt presents the Teacher as a weak but implicitly good man,

so Claire's hard, abrupt and coarse rejection, 'die Welt machte mich
zu einer Hure, nun mache ich sie zu einem Bordell' (p.119/p.91), is
all the more dramatically effective. It turns the Teacher's noble plea
into ideological claptrap.

This scene is one of the many examples in this play which
illustrate the difficulty of directing a Dürrenmatt play. We know that
we are to be dealing with a 'tragischen Komödie' — the subtitle of
the work — and both of these aspects must be kept under
consideration. In this scene, as in many others, the director has to
decide how much 'Tragik' and how much 'Komödie' he will allow.
He can make great comic play with Claire's inappropriate position in
her sedan chair, with the Teacher and the Doctor, sweat-laden — a
favourite Dürrenmatt topos, as I have noted (78, p.217) — trying to
find a seat among the old farm implements; on the other hand, he
must emphasize the chilling inevitability bound up with Claire's
rejection of the Teacher's heartfelt plea. The continual juxtaposition
of tragedy and comedy is part of this play's greatness.

The scene now moves to Ill's store, now full of expensive
goods and with a new and pompous bell, like the church's. We
observe the struggle of the villagers, still denying to each other any
thought of killing Ill, to keep the truth in their hearts from the tape-
recorders and notebooks of the prying pressmen who, unlike their
1990s counterparts, seem only too willing to believe in the goodness
of their victims. Clearly, however, all the conversations show that
the decision has been taken: the Painter presents Frau Ill with
Alfred's portrait which she will hang up over Alfred's bed; she
remarks chillingly: 'Alfred wird alt'; Hofbauer buys himself an axe
and the two elegant women admire the new store and its expensive
goods. (In the 1980 version, the painter has only painted a 'Christus'
(p.95).)

Only the Teacher, after his experience in the barn with Claire,
feels that he must protest in front of the journalists when they arrive,
but he needs copious intakes of schnaps to find the courage to do so.
'Ungeheuerliche Dinge bereiten sich vor in Güllen!' he cries, but his
protest is weakened when he justifies it by adding: 'Denn ich bin ein
Humanist, ein Freund der alten Griechen, ein Bewunderer Platos'

(p.131/p.99). It is perhaps these words, spoken just as Alfred makes his unexpected appearance from his room above, where he has been pacing anxiously back and forth, which make him tell the Teacher to be silent. The irrelevance of the classical ideals to modern cynicism and greed strikes home and, after the comic charade of the enforced happy family picture for the pressmen — 'strahlen vor Glück, strahlen, strahlen, zufrieden, innerlich, stillvergnügt strahlen' (p.133/p.100), we realize that the Teacher's well-meant plea that Alfred should confess all to the pressmen is superfluous when Alfred makes clear that he has come to acknowledge his guilt. This is the intellectual climax of the play: in the classical manner of tragedy, as laid down in Aristotle's *Poetics*, Alfred (the 'hero') is made to recognize that 'great error on his part' (known as *hamartia*) which will allow him to 'fall' in order to restore what Dürrenmatt called 'die verlorene Weltordnung' in his *Theaterprobleme* (WA24, p.63). Like the protagonists of classical tragedy, Ill will be punished for his wrongdoing. The audience should now feel 'pity and sorrow' that a great man has fallen from high estate, and thus the play should have a cathartic effect. But this is not a classical play and Alfred's acknowledgement does not make him a true classical hero, for, as Dürrenmatt makes clear in his *Anmerkung*, his death is 'sinnvoll und sinnlos zugleich' — it would only make sense in a true classical context, 'im mythischen Reich einer antiken Polis', in a realm with a fixed moral code by which all men lived by agreement (p.189/p.143). In the moral mire of Güllen, a stinking mire of cynicism, hypocrisy, fear and greed, Alfred's death will be 'senseless'; he will die, as so many have died, in this 'Wurstelei unseres Jahrhunderts' (*Theaterprobleme*, WA24, p.62) a victim of man's inhumanity to man, a symbol of the many human sacrifices to Mammon.

'Ich habe Klara zu dem gemacht, was sie ist, und mich zu dem, was ich bin, ein verschmierter windiger Krämer', says Alfred (p.137/p.102), and this in turn makes the drunken Teacher realize the hopelessness and uselessness of all his high ideals: he too will 'mitmachen' with the Güllener and help to kill Alfred: 'Die Versuchung ist zu groß und unsere Armut zu bitter' (p.137/p.103), but, unlike the others, he will 'mitmachen' in the sure and certain knowledge that Nemesis will one day come to Güllen for its sin, 'daß auch zu uns einmal eine alte Dame kommen wird' (p.139/P.103).

His action contrasts strongly with that of the Mayor who now tries to make Alfred commit suicide and avoid the scandal which would inconvenience the Güllener. But Alfred, now sure of his moral stand, informs the Mayor that he is prepared to accept the town's judgment in public and to go to his death: 'Für mich ist es die Gerechtigkeit, was es für euch ist, weiß ich nicht' (p.147/p.109). He knows that the Mayor will arrange for the judgment to be couched in hypocritical verbiage which will conceal its true nature, and, although the Mayor's parting shot — that Alfred has lost his chance to become 'ein halbwegs anständiger Mensch' — is meant to wound, the audience will feel that Alfred has won the day.

From this point, the play moves on to its great and inexorable climax in the Theatersaal (pp.161-79/pp.118-31). Alfred's last conversation with Claire in their Konradsweilerwald reveals the agony which Claire suffered at the death of their illegitimate child, but also her true and constant love for Alfred: she has always loved only him, and now she wants him in the only way that she can have him — dead in his coffin which she will now take back with her to Capri.

> Heav'n has no rage, like love to hatr'd turn'd
> Nor Hell a fury, like a woman scorn'd

wrote William Congreve in his play *The Old Bachelor* (1693). It is interesting that the author has made Claire more bitter in the later 1980 version: 'Ich liebte dich,' she says. 'Du hast mich verraten,' but her billions will 'die Vergangenheit ändern, indem ich dich vernichte' (p.117). In the Routledge edition, Claire recalls more sentimentally that Alfred will remain only 'ein toter Geliebter in meiner Erinnerung' (p.161).

And so to the final scene in the theatre hall of Claire's hotel, the Golden Apostle. It is held under the banner 'Ernst ist das Leben, heiter die Kunst', a parody of the closing lines of the prologue to

Schiller's *Wallenstein* and meant to mock the hypocrisy of the proceedings below, set in motion by the radio reporter (these were pre-TV days) who continues in the obsequious manner known from previous scenes. The press has clearly been hoodwinked into believing that what they see and hear is the truth — we are still in the age when the press accepted what an establishment wanted them to hear. Times have changed.

What follows is a fine example of Dürrenmatt's paradoxical theatre. Each speech, each action is ambiguous: the Mayor presents Claire's 'gift' as a contribution from the daughter of their distinguished citizen, Gottfried Wäscher — who we know built the decrepit toilet at the station — towards one of the greatest social experiments of the age, as the reporter puts it. When the Teacher is asked to speak, we hear that he has decided to go along with the Establishment and claim, not that Güllen is accepting the money out of greed, but that it has agreed with Claire's demand for justice: 'Sie will, daß sich unser Gemeinwesen in ein gerechtes verwandle' (p.165/p.121). Although the Teacher refers directly here to the 'injustice' that has occurred in Güllen, when 'die Ehe beleidigt, ein Gericht getäuscht, eine junge Mutter ins Elend gestoßen wird' (p.165/p.121), he now (but hypocritically) begs the Gülleners only to accept the money if they can no longer bear to live in a world of injustice. The reporter takes the Teacher's plea as an example of 'sittliche Größe' and accepts that every community would be bound to have 'Mißstände' and 'Ungerechtigkeiten'. The reporter's interjections when Alfred is asked to stand up, only deepen the sense of ambiguity and hypocrisy, for he announces that Ill is the man responsible for the granting of the gift through his youthful friendship with Claire.

Since no one will query the Mayor's announcement of the decision to accept the money, he proceeds to the arch-hypocritical swearing of the oath which may well be a parody of the celebrated Swiss *Rütli-Schwur* (cf. 29, p.50); the offer will be accepted, he claims, not for the money but for justice: 'Denn wir können nicht leben, wenn wir ein Verbrechen unter uns dulden' (p.171/p.125).

Only at the end of that scene is the whole charade recalled to reality when Ill, horrified at the shameful proceedings, cries out agonisingly, again in biblical terms, 'Mein Gott!' (Jesus cried out 'Mein Gott, mein Gott, warum hast du mich verlassen?' as he was crucified, Matthew 27. 46.) The wonderful *coup de théâtre* which follows has become justly famous in theatrical history: the film camera has failed to function and the cameraman begs them all to repeat the charade, which of course the Mayor and the townspeople are able and willing to do, but which Ill cannot, for his cry was genuine.

Appropriately for Güllen's shame, the final scene takes place behind closed doors and curtains, with the stage lit only by moonlight, a borrowing, no doubt, from the scene of Mani's death in *Mondfinsternis*. There, however, I suggested, was a scene of comical greatness as the villagers waited for the full moon's eclipse before murdering Mani, and in the 1980 version of the play, the *Mond* becomes a *Vollmond*. Here, there is little forced or unforced humour as the Clergyman tries once more to save Alfred's soul by offering to pray for him: 'Beten Sie für Güllen', is Alfred's realistic response as he is pushed into the line of Güllener at the end of which stands the gymnast 'in eleganten weißen Hosen'. Just as Mani is found dead as the moon's light reappears, so too Alfred lies dead — strangled by the gymnast — as the stage lights go up and the pressmen rush in. We recall Claire's instruction to the Doctor in Act I when he pronounces 'Herzschlag'; the Mayor, hypocritical to the last, intones 'Tod aus Freude'.

When Claire reappears, the audience is seeing her for the first time since the scene with Alfred in the wood, but they know what she is going to do. She sees him as he was: 'Er ist wieder so, wie er war, vor langer Zeit' (p.179/p.131), her human black panther, now lying dead, as the symbolic animal lay dead in front of Alfred's own door. She leaves for Capri as promised, and hands the Mayor the cheque for a billion.

The final scene (*Das Schlußbild*) is a parody of the celebrated Chorus of Theban Elders from Sophocles' play *Antigone*, the third of the *Theban Plays* (the others are *King Oedipus* and *Oedipus at*

Colonus) which deals with the battle to the death between Oedipus'
sons, Eteocles and Polynices, and the subsequent death of Oedipus'
daughter, Antigone, at the hands of the demagogue, Creon. (The
Oedipus myth will be discussed again in my examination of *Die
Physiker*).

The Chorus begins (in Friedrich Hölderlin's nineteenth-century
German translation):

> Ungeheuer ist viel. Doch nichts
> Ungeheurer, als der Mensch.

> (Wonders are many on earth, and the greatest of these
> Is man)

and it goes on to declare that man, great though he is, must act
within the bounds and restraints of the moral code:

> But he that, too rashly daring, walks in sin
> In solitary pride to his life's end,
> At door of mine shall never enter in
> To call me friend. (*74*, pp.135-36)[8]

Thus, where Sophocles' chorus teaches the chastened to be
wise, Dürrenmatt's Gülllener (like Max Frisch's Biedermann and his
wife) have clearly learned nothing, and revel in their ill-gotten gains.
But Dürrenmatt warns in his interview *Friedrich Dürrenmatt
interviewt F.D.*:

> Wie der Held der griechischen Tragödie ist die
> Hauptperson (von dem *Besuch der alten Dame*) als der

---

[8]The Chor I's statement 'Ungeheuer ist viel/Gewaltige Erdbeben [...] Der
sonnenhafte Pilz der Atombombe' is answered by Chor II's 'Doch nichts ist
ungeheurer als die Armut', and we realize that Dürrenmatt has answered (or
parodied) Sophocles' positive 'ungeheuer' (meaning 'great' or 'wondrous')
with his own negative 'ungeheuer', meaning 'monstrous' or 'terrible'. His
Chor depicts the evil and not the good in human beings.

'Einzelne' schuldig, doch nachdem der Einzelne seine Schuld eingesehen hat und durch seinen Tod gesühnt hat, wird die Gesellschaft, die bei Sophokles durch den Vollzug der Gerechtigkeit am Einzelnen mit entsühnt wird, nun schuldig. Bei Sophokles weicht die Pest zurück, bei F.D. kommt sie erst; bei Sophokles ist der Einzelne ein Teil des Allgemeinen, bei F.D. nicht (WA25, p.149)

The two choruses in the final scene, resplendent in evening dress, parade about their now prosperous town singing the joys of prosperity in a 'Welt-Happy-End'. They wave farewell to Claire, her retinue and the coffin, with no sign of guilt, sorrow or repentance. They, like so many of Dürrenmatt's 'targeted characters', have learned nothing from Ill's sacrifice — material greed dominates their thinking — but, just as the Teacher warned them that, one day, an old lady might come to them, so too the closing lines of the 'ode' throw an ominous shadow:

Nacht bleibe fern
  Verdunkele nimmermehr unsere Stadt
Die neuerstandene prächtige
  Damit wir das Glück glücklich genießen, (p.185/p.134)

but *we* know that night must fall.

While always bearing in mind that *Der Besuch der alten Dame* was written in the social, economic and political conditions obtaining in 1955-56, it is fair to ask why the play and its theme can be considered timeless. There is no one simple answer to the question, of course, but one might suggest that it is timeless because its major theme is relevant for all ages and for all sorts and conditions of men: that 'the love of money is the root of all evil' (I Timothy 6. 10). Dürrenmatt shows a simple man, Alfred, being sacrificed by a hypocritical society paying lip-service to traditional, now outworn, cultural values and driven on by greed and expectation.

We do not believe that the characters are just cardboard grotesques as is often claimed by those who have never seen, or had to produce, the play on the stage. There Claire is an awesome personality, fearsome too in her comic, inhuman monstrosity, wreaking her revenge for the wrong done to her forty-five years previously. Her body, now made of spare parts, symbolically represents the deformation of the human race in the twentieth century, degraded by its lusts. She stands, symbolically but also literally, outside the action, yet directing it, like some antique goddess who treats the Güllener as her puppets, and they in turn respond like puppets, with their stylized speech patterns and gestures, as in the early scene at the station, and later, when they act as trees in the Konradsweilerwald.

Not that Alfred is a cardboard character. He is the only one in the play to produce a genuine human reaction and response; he sees the error of his ways and accepts the supreme punishment. His reactions to Claire and to the hypocritical assurances of the Mayor and his colleagues evoke sympathy in the audience who see, not a dastardly evil seducer, but a normal 'little man' — 'ein gedankenloses Mannsbild', as Dürrenmatt described him in the *Anmerkung* — paying so fully for what seems to have been his only crime; 'an sich erlebt er die Gerechtigkeit, weil er seine Schuld erkennt, er wird groß durch sein Sterben...' (p.189/p.143). In that sense, this play is Dürrenmatt's only true 'tragicomedy' in that, in Alfred, we do have a tragic character in a comic situation. The Knapps were therefore accurate when they called *Der Besuch der alten Dame* 'eine Tragikomödie des Wirtschaftswunders' (*58*, p.27).

In his later works, Dürrenmatt began to see characters like Alfred Ill as 'Einzelne', as isolated characters caught in their own labyrinth, misunderstood by the world in which they lived.[9] We see them as autobiographical characters, sketched by a man who, as his life wore on, felt increasingly cut off from his public and fellow-

[9]Towards the end of his life, Dürrenmatt wrote a great deal on the motif of the labyrinth. See *78*, pp.205-08 for a full discussion of the theme in, for example, his *Minotaurus. Eine Ballade* (1985). See too *61*, p.47, where the von Zahnd asylum is likened to Möbius' 'labyrinth'.

writers alike, cut off by his physical ill health, by his physical isolation from German-speakers in Neuchâtel, and from other German writers by his 'Swiss-ness'. His firmly held belief that the world was being despoiled by economic greed and technological pollution, the results of man's hubris (his overweening arrogance), is the theme of most of his works.

5. *The Background to* Die Physiker

The six years between the production of *Der Besuch der alten Dame* and the astounding premiere(s) of *Die Physiker* in the same theatre, the Schauspielhaus Zürich, on three successive nights, 20-22 February 1962, had seen Friedrich Dürrenmatt established as one of the world's leading playwrights. *Der Besuch der alten Dame* was produced all over the world, including London and New York, and had been translated into many languages, which encouraged his publisher, the Peter Schifferli Verlag, 'Die Arche', to create a house-style for the author's works, blue-tooled books inscribed with the simple signature 'Dürrenmatt'.

These six years were also the years of a growing intensification of the Cold War, that symbol of the pathological, mutual hatred between the USA and the USSR, and the division of the world into two ideological camps, capitalism versus communism. The release in 1993 of the British Cabinet's secret papers for these years show how near to nuclear catastrophe the world came between 1960 and 1962, when the youthful and impetuous president of the United States, John F. Kennedy, was tested almost beyond endurance by the Soviet president Nikita Khrushchev's obstinate plans to build nuclear bases on the island of Cuba, Fidel Castro's communist stronghold, within striking distance of the USA. The then British prime minister, Harold Macmillan, did his utmost to restrain the impulsive young president, and his and others' entreaties eventually prevailed on both leaders — Khrushchev finally yielding to the US naval blockade in October 1962. Dürrenmatt was writing *Die Physiker* in 1961 just at the time of the celebrated and unsuccessful 'Bay of Pigs' incident, when 1,500 anti-Castro Cuban exiles, backed by Kennedy and the CIA, tried to invade Cuba on 17-20 April 1961. Of the 1,500, 1,173 were taken prisoner.

In that same month the Soviets proclaimed the (seeming) technological superiority of the Marxist system when their folk hero, Yuri Gagarin, became the first human being to fly in space; and the world became physically divided when the infamous Berlin Wall (the *Schandmauer*) was erected on 13 August 1961, dividing the former German capital into hostile zones, and proving, incidentally, that Marxism did not have the overwhelming public support that the Soviets claimed. When we recall too that France announced the testing of its first atomic bomb in the Sahara in 1961 (following the American tests on the Bikini Atoll in the Pacific in 1954), then it will be appreciated how a writer, as interested in science as Dürrenmatt had been all his life, would consider a literary response. We know from recollections of his early life in *Labyrinth* how fascinated he had always been by physics: 'Die Physik begann mich zu faszinieren,' he wrote about his youthful days preparing for his *Maturität* (the equivalent of Advanced Level) in Berne, 'zum ersten Mal ahnte ich, was exakte Begriffe bedeuten: nicht eine Wahrheit, die gänzlich unabhängig vom Menschen wäre, im Gegenteil, aber eine Wahrheit, die es nur dank der Vernunft gibt, von ihr kunstvoll und oft listenreich erstellt, eine "menschliche Wahrheit" ' (*8*, pp.212-13. See too above p.21). That he, like almost all of his generation, still lived under the shadow of that atomic cloud which had devastated the Japanese towns of Hiroshima, on 6 August 1945, and Nagasaki, three days later, at a cost of over 300,000 lives and countless subsequent genetic tragedies, had been noted at the end of his *Theaterprobleme* where he wrote: 'Unsere Welt hat ebenso zur Groteske geführt wie zur Atombombe' (WA24, p.62), and earlier, in a typical Dürrenmattian linguistic flash of wit: 'Die Atombombe kann man nicht mehr darstellen, seit man sie herstellen kann. Vor ihr versagt jede Kunst als eine Schöpfung des Menschen, weil sie selbst eine Schöpfung des Menschen ist' (WA24, p.60).

Indeed, it was just such a feeling of helplessness which had led many contemporary writers into abandoning the old conventions of tragedy on the stage and adopting a form of theatre which expressed this helplessness in an outward show of, in both senses of the word, 'helpless' laughter concealing a deep and fearsome sense of tragedy.

The 'sense of metaphysical anguish at the absurdity of the human condition' (often labelled with the Kafkaesque word 'Angst') led the critic Martin Esslin to write his seminal book *The Theatre of the Absurd* (*32*) in that very year 1961. In it he quoted (in English translation) the French writer Albert Camus who wrote in his *Le Mythe de Sisyphe* in 1942:

> Un monde qu'on peut expliquer même avec de mauvaises raisons est un monde familier. Mais au contraire, dans un univers soudain privé d'illusions et de lumières, l'homme se sent un étranger.[10]

Although that was written in 1942, it was generally felt that it explained the absence of rationality and of purpose in life which was so evident to the intellectuals of the '60s. Significantly perhaps, only Max Frisch and his *Biedermann und die Brandstifter* (1958) are cited as one of the 'parallels and proselytes' in the first edition of Esslin's book. Dürrenmatt is mentioned only as a compatriot of Frisch who, like him, used a dramatic idiom which 'owes a great deal to Bernard Shaw', with its vein of 'disillusioned tragicomedy' (*32*, pp.198-99). Dürrenmatt was no lover of the absurd and called it once 'ein leichtfertiger Begriff' in one of my conversations (*77*, p.18), while in conversation with Martin Esslin in 1963, he claimed that his theatre was a 'theatre of paradox' which showed the 'paradoxical results of strict logic', and this required 'extreme rationality in structure and dialogue' (*31*, pp.15-16). I shall return to this important point later.

In my introductory chapter on *Der Besuch der alten Dame* I noted that Dürrenmatt claimed that his plots arose from a mixture of 'Erleben, Phantasie und Stoff' (see above, p.21); if the political world situation, as just described, was the *Erlebnis*, then the 'Phantasie und Stoff' were his musings on the theme of the Greek tragic hero Oedipus. Dürrenmatt was well versed in Greek tragedy; his clergyman father read Greek and Latin fluently and regularly, and related the Greek legends to his son at every opportunity. As

---

[10]Camus, Albert, *Le Mythe de Sisyphe: essai sur l'absurde*, Folio Essais (Paris, Gallimard, 1985), p.20.

Dürrenmatt developed his belief in the primacy of chance ('Zufall') in human affairs, the Oedipus myth became for him the supreme example of that philosophical tenet which the philosopher-physicist Werner Heisenberg had once termed the *Principle of Indeterminacy*.[11]

Oedipus, it will be recalled, was the son of Laius and Jocasta, but even before a name could be given to the infant 'Apollo's oracle had nothing but ill to foretell of him; he was destined one day to kill his father and to become his own mother's husband' (*74*, p.23). The parents delivered the child to a shepherd with orders to abandon it on the mountainside, its feet cruelly pierced with an iron pin to prevent its crawling to safety. But the shepherd could not bear to leave the child, and gave it to a Corinthian shepherd to take it as far away from Thebes as possible. Polybus, the childless King of Corinth welcomed the infant with delight and adopted it under the name of Oedipus, Latin for 'swollen feet'. Oedipus grew to manhood, heard of Apollo's oracle, but, like his parents, decided to defy it, and fled from Corinth to wander the world. These wanderings brought him back to his own country of Thebes where, after an altercation with a traveller (whom he later killed) on the road, he destroyed a deadly monster, the Sphinx, which was terrorising the country. Unaware that the man whom he had killed on the lonely road had been the King of Thebes (his own father, Laius), Oedipus accepted the Thebans' gratitude, was proclaimed king and took the queen (Jocasta, his own mother) as his wife who then bore him two sons and two daughters. When Oedipus eventually discovered the awful truth, he pierced his own eyes and blinded himself. Jocasta committed suicide, and Oedipus was led away to be banished from Thebes, thus fulfilling the oracle's prophecy.

For Dürrenmatt this seemed to be a perfect example of the workings of chance. He said once of the Oedipus myth:

---

[11]Werner Heisenberg (1901-76) was the originator of quantum mechanics. His *Principle* laid down that there was a limit to physical measurement in experiments because the very act of measurement changed the behaviour of the objects being measured. His attempt to find a natural law accounting for the existence of all atomic particles failed.

> Ein Mensch erfährt durch ein Orakel sein Schicksal. Und
> er wird nun dazu gezwungen, diesem Schicksal entgehen
> zu wollen, wodurch er gerade diesem Schicksal
> entgegenläuft. Seine Flucht ist ein Hineingehen in sein
> Schicksal. (*61*, p.46)

That is to say, in Dürrenmatt's view, fate was determined by the
gods, but Oedipus' attempt to escape that fate, i.e. a human attempt,
exposed him to the workings of blind, ineluctable chance. It was
chance which brought him home from his wanderings back to
Thebes; chance which brought about the meeting with, and the
murder of, the lonely traveller, his father Laius; chance which led to
his crowning as King of Thebes and to the marriage with Jocasta, his
mother. In other words, Dürrenmatt parodies classical fate as modern
chance. Fate is a matter of the gods' omniscience; chance is a matter
of man's limitations. In his foreword to his story *Die Panne*,
Dürrenmatt wrote:

> Das Schicksal hat die Bühne verlassen, auf der gespielt
> wird, um hinter den Kulissen zu lauern, außerhalb der
> gültigen Dramaturgie, im Vordergrund wird alles zum
> Unfall, die Krankheiten, die Krisen. (WA20, p.39)

Dürrenmatt's belief in the workings of 'Zufall' was, of course, a
direct refutation of the Calvinist beliefs of his clergyman father; the
Calvinist-Lutheran belief that God predetermines all events and that
the individual soul is 'pre-elected' to glory or perdition frightened the
young Dürrenmatt, and his distancing of himself from this belief was
synonymous with his distancing himself from his mother from
whom, he wrote later, he felt separated by a 'Mauer aus Glauben'
(*Labyrinth*, *8*, p.189). 'Die Religion wurde mir peinlich, ich
mißtraute ihr und hatte ein schlechtes Gewissen' (*8*, p.193). I believe
therefore that self-knowledge of bad conscience and of personal guilt
is a *sine qua non* for a true understanding of Dürrenmatt's works.

Dürrenmatt's tenet that the world is governed by chance and
not by an iron fate merged with his thoughts on the disastrous

inability of the world's finest logical thinkers to foresee the consequences of the construction of the atom bomb. They, like Oedipus, he reasoned, had committed themselves to an action which they could not 'unthink' or retract, and which had catastrophic consequences. These thoughts were deepened when he had to review in 1956 *Heller als tausend Sonnen: Das Schicksal der Atomforscher*, the story of how the atom bomb came into being. The name of the author was Robert Jungk, the pseudonym of a Jewish refugee, Dr Robert Baum. In his review, printed originally in the Zürich *Weltwoche* on 7 December 1956 (and now in WA28, pp.20-24), Dürrenmatt called the book 'eine Chronik vom Untergang einer Welt der reinen Vernunft', a reference to Immanuel Kant's *Kritik der reinen Vernunft* of 1781. Jungk argued that the building of the bomb could have been prevented had the twelve physicists, engaged in the Manhattan Project in 1939, decided against continuing the work. However, because they believed that the Germans were also making a bomb (which they were not), the Hungarian physicist Szilard persuaded Albert Einstein to talk the American president, Franklin D. Roosevelt, into entering into a competition which, in fact, never existed. Thus, according to Dürrenmatt, the bomb was constructed by an 'internationalen Elite von Wissenschaftlern' (we note the phrase) urged on by contemporary politicians. There was no chance for these scientists 'Denkbares geheim zu behalten', and since every scientific process is repeatable, the scientists had delivered their knowledge into the hands of power politicians 'aus dem Reiche der reinen Vernunft in jenes der Realität'. From this Dürrenmatt deduced that the major question for the future would be: 'Wie sich die Physiker in der heutigen Welt verhalten müssen' for, as he continued, their mistake was: 'Das Wissen fürchtete sich vor der Macht und lieferte sich deshalb den Mächten aus.'

It is interesting to note how the figure of Albert Einstein has continued to fascinate Dürrenmatt. Einstein (1879-1955) was born in Ulm in Germany of Jewish stock, but took Swiss citizenship and taught physics at the University of Zürich at intervals between 1909 and 1912. He was therefore of special interest to a Swiss author fascinated by physics. Long after writing *Die Physiker* Dürrenmatt was invited to give an important lecture on Einstein in the physicist's former research building in the Eidgenössischen Technischen Hochschule in Zürich on 24 February 1979. Dürrenmatt perhaps significantly prefaced the written form of the lecture with a biblical quotation: 'Habe ich wirklich geirrt, so trage ich meinen Irrtum selbst' ('And be it indeed that I have erred, mine error remaineth with myself', Job 19. 4). However, the chapter goes on to show how Job has been disgraced and rejected: 'Be ye afraid of the sword: for wrath bringeth the punishments of the sword, that ye may know there is a judgment' (v.29).

Dürrenmatt concluded this lecture by suggesting that Einstein was one of those thinkers who had led the 'Rebellion gegen das Chaos' but who, paradoxically, by his *Special Theory of Relativity* of 1905 (where $E=mc^2$, E being mass energy, m mass and c^2 the square of the speed of light), had supplied the conditions for the transfer of mass into energy and the construction of the atomic bomb. He cited Einstein's pathetic 'O weh' when he heard of the consequences in Japan in 1945 as 'von einer unendlichen Hilflosigkeit' (WA27, pp.150-72). Instead of leading mankind to a view of 'einer prästabilisierten Harmonie', Einstein and his fellow-scientists had led the world to a 'Vision einer prästabilisierten Explosion'. The supreme irony for Dürrenmatt is, of course, that Einstein's academic researches were conditioned by intuition and not by formal logical mathematical processes, and that his failure to find 'eine allgemine Feldtheorie' resulted from his inadequate knowledge of advanced mathematics, the quintessence of logical thinking. It should be noted too how Einstein's 'allgemeine Relativitätstheorie' and his 'Gravitationstheorie', published after his move from Zürich to Berlin in 1919, were considered to have replaced Sir Isaac Newton's *Universal Law of Gravitation* as formulated in his *Philosophiae Naturalis Principia Mathematica* of 1686-87. We shall see how Dürrenmatt used these facts in his portrayal of the main characters in his play.

One last major point remains to be considered: Dürrenmatt was not, of course, the only major author to consider what we have called a 'literary response' to the awesome question of the effects of the discovery of nuclear fission and the atomic bomb. After him came Heinar Kipphardt with his interesting play *In der Sache J. Robert Oppenheimer* in 1964, a good example of the then popular 'documentary theatre'. The play dealt with social and political questions by reproducing the actual trial of the American physicist. However, before Dürrenmatt there had of course been the response from Germany's leading writer, Bertolt Brecht. The relationship between Dürrenmatt and Brecht has been closely examined, but of particular interest to this study is their treatment of the theme under discussion.[12] Where Dürrenmatt chose to portray the later protagonists, Newton and Einstein, Brecht in the first version of his *Leben des Galilei* went back to the life of the founder of theoretical physics, Galileo Galilei (1564-1642), his destruction of Ptolemy's — and the Catholic Church's — cosmological theories and his formulation of the *Law of Gravitation*, later refined by Newton. Galilei, because of his recantation before the Inquisition of his theory that the earth went round the sun, was for Brecht a traitor to the cause of science and society. It was the 'Sündenfall der bürgerlichen Wissenschaft am Beginn ihres Aufstiegs'.

In 1945-46 *Galilei* was translated into English by Brecht and the British actor Charles Laughton and, while working on this version, Brecht learned of the dropping of the atomic bomb on Japan: 'Von heute auf morgen,' he wrote, 'las sich die Biografie des Begründers der neuen Physik anders'; and the third version of the play (1956) makes Galilei not only a traitor but also a criminal: 'Am Schluß ist er ein Förderer der Wissenschaft und ein sozialer Verbrecher [...] er unterliegt der Versuchung der Wissenschaft,' Brecht said during one of the rehearsals of the play. Martin Esslin then showed how, for Galilei, 'the urge for knowledge, the most rational side of human endeavour, science itself, is shown as being merely another of man's basic, instinctive urges [...]. To be able to indulge this instinct, Galilei is prepared to commit the meanest

---

[12]See my 79 and also Knapp (57), Mayer (62), Morley (63), Roe (69) and Rülicke-Weiler (72).

action.'[13] During that rehearsal mentioned above, Brecht went on to say: 'Das ist eine der großen Schwierigkeiten: aus dem Helden den Verbrecher herauszuholen. Trotzdem: er ist ein Held und trotzdem: er wird zum Verbrecher.' Käthe Rülicke-Weiler adds: 'Diese Situation des Galilei ermöglichte Parallelen zur Gegenwart' (72, pp.232-312). Brecht's parallels (in 1956) were what he saw as the new dangers from a powerful, anti-communist West; Dürrenmatt's parallels (as we shall see) were the biblical 'beasts' that dwell in every man.

Brecht, a convinced Marxist, who, after seven years' exile in the USA, returned to the newly-founded *Deutsche Demokratische Republik* in Berlin in 1948-49, was thus writing the third version of *Galilei* at the outset of the Cold War. For him Western, and particularly American, science was dooming the world to a catastrophic future: scientists must understand that their discoveries must be tempered by the knowledge that their 'Jubelschrei über irgend eine neue Errungenschaft von einem universalen Entsetzensschrei beantwortet werden könnte' (*Leben des Galilei*, Scene 14).

Dürrenmatt's *Die Physiker* could therefore be seen as proof that he was simply a 'Nachfolger' of the great Brecht. The Swiss writer denied this vehemently, above all in his lecture *Friedrich Schiller* of 1959 when he compared the eighteenth-century German classic with himself, and Brecht. He demonstrated there his dislike of Brecht's dogmatic Marxist pronouncements and, above all, of Brecht's belief that the world can be changed by men's actions: 'Der alte Glaubenssatz der Revolutionäre, daß der Mensch die Welt verändern könne und müsse, ist für den einzelnen unrealisierbar geworden,' he wrote. It is only a 'Schlagwort', 'politisches Dynamit' for the masses (in WA26, pp.82-102). (Brecht's Kontrollchor in his play *Die Maßnahme*, 1930, had cried out: 'Ändre die Welt, sie braucht es'. See *79*.)

I believe that Dürrenmatt's pronouncements on Brecht's over-optimistic Marxist beliefs in the 'communist heaven' were true then

---

[13]Esslin, M., *Brecht: A Choice of Evils*, 4th, rev. ed. (London, Methuen, 1984), p.234.

and are even truer today after the collapse of the Eastern communist dictatorships. It does not make Dürrenmatt a capitalist pessimist but rather a realist who sees that human nature has never changed since the world began: man has always been tempted by greed and selfishness; the struggle for us all is to fight these temptations; it is unlikely that we shall conquer all of them, but we might, by concerted action, make their efforts less dreadful. 'Jeder Versuch eines Einzelnen, für sich zu lösen, was alle angeht, muß scheitern' (*Die Physiker*, Point 18). To do that, however, we must ensure that the individual has his freedom, freedom to choose the right path, the 'narrow way' of the Bible (Matthew 7. 14).

6. Die Physiker: *The Introduction and the Minor Characters*

'Jeder Mensch ist ein Weltmittelpunkt für sich selber, und zweitens ist er ein Wesen, eingegliedert in eine Gesellschaft. Das ist der Urkonflikt des Menschen überhaupt,' said Dürrenmatt in a conversation with René Sauter in 1966 (73, p.1229), and, curiously, it was Robert Jungk whose book *Heller als tausend Sonnen* Dürrenmatt had reviewed in 1956, who had written of the scientist's problem in today's world; he was 'der gespaltene Mensch', whose work and rediscoveries, representing progress for him and his branch of science, might however bring him into conflict with the society of which he must be part. This was the first 'Einfall' which led to the writing of *Die Physiker*. Dürrenmatt told us much later how, while he was fighting the dread diabetes from which he had suffered all his life, he was incarcerated in 1959 in a sanatorium (Waldhaus Vulpera) in the Unterengadin in Switzerland. There, no matter what treatment or what diet he received, the 'Tes-Tape-Streifen' by which diabetes sufferers know whether or not they need more insulin, remained always green, a fatal sign: 'Der Tod hat für mich ein grünes Gesicht,' Dürrenmatt wrote in *Turmbau* (7, p.32). He was ordered to walk as much as possible, and it was on one of his walks that the idea of writing *Die Physiker* and the later play *Der Meteor* (1966), the theme of which is death, occurred to him. Perhaps, he wrote, the ominous tape reminded him of the Delphic oracle which so upset Oedipus that he fled to Thebes — to his doom. Like Oedipus, Dürrenmatt continued, Möbius in *Die Physiker* knew his fate too, not because of any oracle, but because, as a scientist, he knew what could happen because of his discoveries: 'Wie Ödipus will auch Möbius seinem Schicksal entgehen.' But like Oedipus he chooses the wrong path and flees into the wrong asylum. And Dürrenmatt

himself? 'Wem der Tes-Tape-Streifen grün wird, weiß sein Schicksal
auch' (7, p.33) — a revealing comment for those who know how
much the disease has influenced the author's life and career.

It is important that theatre programmes for a performance of
Die Physiker should print Dürrenmatt's extensive introduction, four
pages long in Volume 7 of the *Werkausgabe*. It explains the
dramaturgical thinking behind the play and supplies 'clues' which
encourage the audience or the reader to think, to 'make connections',
during the performance or the reading of what is really a detective
story. Dürrenmatt, whose greatest joy was making fun of rituals and
cutting down to size or deflating pompous characters and
institutions, fills this introduction with pointed and witty comments.

We find ourselves in the lounge in the villa of a rather decrepit
private sanatorium, 'Les Cerisiers' ('The Cherry Wood'). Those who
know Dürrenmatt's predilection for 'versteckte Namen' (see above,
pp.30-31) will think immediately of the favourite Swiss drink *Kirsch*
(*Chriesi* in Schwyzertütsch), or cherry brandy; those who know
Dürrenmatt's literary forebears might think of Chekhov's play *The
Cherry Orchard* of 1904 (in French, *La Cerisaie*) with its doomed
and ineffectual characters. The general picture is of a run-down,
desolate area near a lake and a smallish town, with little more to
offer than a modest university of which the main claims to fame are
a theological faculty and summer language courses. There are also a
commercial college, a dental technicians' college and a home for
female old-age pensioners. Nothing could be further from the worlds
of high tech and big business. But more: the landscape is also just as
desolate — mountains, a lake and a darkening moor on which are
working prisoners from a nearby institution. As in *Der Besuch der
alten Dame* we are inclined to take all the hints of names and places
to indicate that we are in Switzerland: 'Les Cerisiers', 'Jung', 'Ernis
Glasmalereien' (Hans Erni, born 1909 in Switzerland, reintroduced
the tradition of decorating Swiss houses with stained-glass
paintings.) The thinly-disguised area of the asylum is obviously the
open area beyond the road where Dürrenmatt's house is situated in
Neuchâtel, where similar institutions are to be found. Nor would
Dürrenmatt be the first Swiss to find the country's obsession with

cleanliness oppressive. This is why so many of his descriptions present unkempt and dirty locations. His friend Peter Rüedi wrote that the irony of these descriptions is typical, 'weil doch das Dreckigste an der Schweiz ihre Sauberkeit ist!' (*71*, p.57).

Immediately however, the author whisks us away from the scene: 'Doch spielt das Örtliche eigentlich keine Rolle' (p.1/p.11), and describes for us the villa of the — and now he lets fall the word — 'Irrenhaus' (literally 'madhouse'), instead of the former, more genteel 'Sanatorium'. The juxtaposition of 'Verbrecher' outside and 'Irrenhaus' inside might indicate that the area is not as innocent, or as devoid of drama, as has been suggested up to this point. The locale, we are now told, will be strictly 'classical' — the so-called Aristotelian Unities of Time, Place and Action will be observed: 'einer Handlung die unter Verrückten spielt, kommt nur die klassische Form bei', an aphorism much quoted during the years of the *Theatre of the Absurd* discussed above.[14]

For Dürrenmatt, of course, this was an extension of his argument in *Theaterprobleme* where, after granting the power and usefulness of the Three Unities, he strove to show that they were no longer valid in the new world of theatre where classical tragedy had been replaced by, firstly, Brecht's Epic Theatre, then by the film and now, according to Dürrenmatt, by the *Komödie*: 'Uns kommt nur noch die Komödie bei,' he wrote in *Theaterprobleme* (WA24, p.62). Here however we are presented with a fine Dürrenmattian paradox — a *Komödie* (the subtitle of the play) but in a classical form which is why Point 14 tells us: 'Ein Drama über die Physiker muß paradox sein' (p.90/p.92). The author now proceeds to give us what in *Theaterprobleme* he termed the 'Vorgeschichte'. He gives us this because we are about to witness a 'classical' plot, but the audiences for a play in Greek times needed no such introduction: 'Die

---

[14] The 'Three Unities' were developed in the sixteenth century from the Aristotelian model by the Italian translator of the *Poetics*, Ludovico Castelvetro (1505-1571); these were later accepted and adapted by the French neo-classical dramatists. The action was to take place within the time of the performance; this was later extended to twenty-four hours. The scene should not change; later, one could move from one point to another within a larger area. There should be no sub-plots.

griechische Tragödie nun lebt von der Möglichkeit, die Vorgeschichte nicht erfinden zu müssen,' because the audience already knew the stories of the great myths. However, if he, a modern author, is to write a plot which should take about two hours to play, 'so muß diese Handlung eine Vorgeschichte haben, und diese Vorgeschichte wird um so größer sein müssen, je weniger Personen mir zur Verfügung stehen' (WA24, pp.34-35).

And so 'zur Sache', as the dramatist suggests. The inmates of the villa are typical of Dürrenmatt's somewhat jaundiced view of modern society: 'vertrottelte Aristokraten, arteriosklerotische Politiker [...], debile Millionäre, schizophrene Schriftsteller, manisch-depressive Großindustrielle [...], die ganze geistig verwirrte Elite des halben Abendlandes' (p.2/p.12), a clientele which might prove to the audience that the director and founder of the asylum, Fräulein Dr h.c. Dr med. Mathilde von Zahnd has fully earned her medical doctor's as well as her honorary degree — but also that it is possible that birds of a feather have flocked together. Her correspondence with the Swiss psychiatrist Carl Gustav Jung (1875-1961) is also not without significance, since Jung was often accused of having introduced irrational and occult influences into his profession. It will be noted too that Jung had just died so that he was a topical issue.

All the other patients have now been moved, we learn, into the elegant and light new building; only three patients — 'zufälligerweise Physiker' (another detective story clue) — remain in the old villa. They are, we are assured, 'harmlose, liebenswerte Irre' who spend their days staring into space and causing no trouble. They would indeed be model patients had not something 'Bedenkliches', indeed 'Gräßliches' occurred: three months ago, one of them had strangled his nurse, and now it has happened again and the police are back in the asylum. This explains, says the author, the untidy scene that would have confronted the audience had the room not been tidied up: a standard lamp, two armchairs and a table lie upturned on the floor, the legs facing the audience, and in the background, decently hidden, the body of the nurse. Obviously a struggle has taken place, but the room itself — with its walls covered with a sort of white hygienic paint which hardly conceals the cement beneath it, an ugly central-heating unit, a washhand basin — all of these betray 'schmerzliche Spuren' of the alteration of the von Zahnd family summer residence into a functional sanatorium-asylum. Further clues to the plot are given by the three doors to the rear, upholstered in black leather and numbered 1 to 3; for out of one of them, number 2, come the civilized strains of a violin and piano playing Beethoven's Opus 47 sonata, the Kreutzer. (It was composed in 1802-03 and dedicated to the French violinist, Rudolphe Kreutzer who died, in Geneva in Switzerland, in 1831). So, once again, a paradox: rational classical music in an asylum in which a seemingly irrational murder has just taken place.

When the curtain rises, it is 4.30 pm on a sunny afternoon in November (often Dürrenmatt's 'dying' month). The sparse furniture ('leicht zerschlissen, verschiedene Epochen') should have been put back in place: 'Zur Ausstattung einer Bühne, auf der, im Gegensatz zu den Stücken der Alten, das Satyrspiel der Tragödie vorangeht, gehört wenig' writes the author. The reference is to the 'satyr play', the forerunner of modern comedy in early Greek drama; these plays came after the normal trilogy of tragedies, often reversing and making mockeries of the tragic plots, thus giving rise to modern satires. So another clue: the author will present us with yet another paradox by inverting the classical model and placing the tragedy after the comedy.

I hold the introduction to be of vital importance, not just for an understanding of *Die Physiker*, but for the insights it affords into Dürrenmatt's dramaturgical technique. In many ways, it is a practical illustration of the theoretical tenets in *Theaterprobleme*. There he wrote: 'Der Einfall verwandelt die Menge der Theaterbesucher besonders leicht in eine Masse, die nun angegriffen, verführt, überlistet werden kann, sich Dinge anzuhören, die sie sich sonst nicht so leicht anhören würde', and he adds, 'Die Komödie ist eine Mausefalle' which will always trap the public (WA24, p.64). Although in Point 21 at the end of *Die Physiker* he adds the timely warning to fellow-dramatists, that even so one cannot force the audience 'ihr [der Wirklichkeit] standzuhalten, oder sie gar zu bewältigen'; we feel that he hopes nevertheless that his *Komödie* will lend support to the anti-nuclear lobby. But when in April 1962, two months after the premieres of his play, the Swiss people voted to support the proposal that they should share in the atomic defence of Europe, the truth of Point 21 was borne out. As he had said shortly before to Horst Bienek in reply to the latter's question 'Can a writer change the world?', 'Beunruhigen im besten, beeinflussen im seltensten Falle, verändern *nie!*' (*19*).

At the end of that introduction Dürrenmatt writes: 'Wir können beginnen', and we now meet the first of the characters in the play. The Police Inspector, Richard Voß, is directing the operations of his men, all in civilian clothes, and on his left stands the Oberschwester, Marta Boll. It has already been suggested that the names in Dürrenmatt's play are as worthy of attention as those in *Der Besuch der alten Dame*; the author would certainly seem to be suggesting this with his comment: 'links Oberschwester Marta Boll, die so resolut aussieht, wie sie heißt und ist', a reference, no doubt, to the noun 'das Bollwerk', the bulwark.

When we look at the *Personenliste*, it is possible to divide the characters into four groups: firstly, the minor characters — the Inspector, the nurses and the Rose Family; secondly, the guards and the policemen; then the scientists, Möbius, and the two physicists, and lastly Fräulein Dr von Zahnd.

To take the minor characters first: the Inspector and the others in this first group are important minor characters who, like the Mayor and the other leading Güllener in *Der Besuch der alten Dame*, are essential to the plot. The Inspector himself is a type well known from TV and film and to readers of Dürrenmatt from many of his prose works which feature policemen: *Der Richter und sein Henker*, *Der Verdacht*, *Das Versprechen* from the 1950s, and from his two later novels *Justiz* (1985) and *Der Auftrag* (1986) — a solid, stolid type whose very lack of a sense of humour makes him a comic figure. When the conversation with Marta Boll begins, not only the diction, but also the unusual type of line-by-line conversation, noted before as *stychomythia* (cf. footnote 1 on p.14), gives a comic effect by making the characters seem puppet-like. Yet Dürrenmatt also achieves a serious purpose from the conversation, since we hear all the details of the murdered nurse, Irene Straub. (It was clear from the description of the condition of the room that the strangled nurse 'sich ge*sträubt* hatte' — my italics.) The Inspector is treated like a child by the resolute nurse, forbidden to smoke or to drink a schnaps, angrily corrected when he calls the assailant 'Der Mörder' instead of 'Der Täter': ('der arme Mensch [Ernst Heinrich Ernesti, the assailant] ist doch krank,' says Sister Boll, p.5/p.15), or when he calls the 'Unglücksfall' a murder.

The comedy of misunderstandings continues when the Inspector tries to interview the accused, and is told: 'Er geigt.' We can hear the sound of Beethoven's music coming from Room 2. We have also heard that the 'sick man' believes himself to be Albert Einstein, 'Und weil er sich für Einstein hält, beruhigt er sich nur, wenn er geigt' (p.7/p.17). The comic inconsequentiality of the remark leads the Inspector to the, in the circumstances, even more comic response: 'Bin ich eigentlich verrückt?' which is followed by what we noted earlier was a typical Dürrenmattian stage direction when a character is non-plussed, embarrassed or deflated: 'Er wischt sich den Schweiß ab' (see 78, p.217 for a discussion of the reasons).

The diction too is intentionally comical. When Blocher, the Policeman, says: 'Wir wären fertig, Herr Inspektor', the disoriented Inspector answers with what is called in German a 'Kalauer', a stale pun: 'Und mich macht man fertig.' Critical opinion has always been divided as to whether Dürrenmatt means these to be poor jokes to establish the character as one who is trying to be funny — or whether Dürrenmatt himself tells poor jokes. There are many in *Die Physiker*, and audiences certainly enjoy them. Critics who do not enjoy them seem to feel themselves personally offended, as, for example, the critic of the *Basler Nachrichten* after the premiere of Dürrenmatt's *Komödie Herkules und der Stall des Augias* with its supremely witty parody of the classical myth, its stage covered with brown brocade to represent the legendary dung ('der Mist'), subject of many of the play's witticisms. He wrote: 'Man kann Mist gewiß an sich und als solchen umwerfend komisch finden, und wird sich

vermutlich beim Spaziergang durch ein Bauerndorf bei jedem
Dunghaufen vor Lachen biegen. Ich kann es nicht.'[15]

We have just heard that Ernesti believes himself to be
Einstein; when Herbert Georg Beutler appears from Room 3 dressed
as, and announcing himself as, Sir Isaac Newton (the 1980 version
has the correct English spelling of the Christian name), the Inspector
is quite taken aback and can only remain seated. Beutler too treats
the Inspector in comic fashion, forbidding him to smoke while
helping himself to a cigarette, and a glass of cognac. The Inspector is
now put in the position of the audience as he tries to fathom the true
nature of the two physicists. Beutler, dressed as Newton, introduces
himself as Newton, then claims that he is only pretending to be
Newton in order not to confuse Ernesti. The Inspector, granted only
a word or two in the conversation, is perplexed. 'Im Gegensatz zu
mir.' says Beutler, 'ist Ernesti doch wirklich krank. Er bildet sich ein,
Albert Einstein zu sein' (p.12/p.21). In the next breath, Beutler
claims that he is actually Einstein and gives a short biography of the
famous physicist.

The Inspector now requires a meeting with only one more
character to prepare the audience for the beginning of the plot. That
character is the director of the institution, Fräulein Doktor Mathilde
von Zahnd, who now makes her entrance. Immediately we are
confronted with a paradox: firstly, where her nurse has refused Voß
permission to smoke, the Director turns a blind eye to his cigarette
and takes one herself — 'Oberschwester Marta hin oder her'
(p.16/p.25). Secondly, she assures Voß that Newton really does think
that he is Newton and not Einstein, and she adds revealingly: 'Für
wen sich meine Patienten halten, bestimme ich' (which many
Germans would take to be a parody of the well-known and chilling
remark of Vienna's famous anti-Semitic mayor (from 1897 to 1910),
Karl Lueger, who once said: 'Wer Jude ist, bestimme ich').

It is then the Inspector who sets the scene for the dénouement
in Act II by demanding that the security measures be strengthened.
The incarceration of the three physicists provides the ground for

---

[15]*Basler Nachrichten*, 21 March 1963. Daniel Keel has published a
collection of Dürrenmatt's witticisms and philosophical *aperçus* in *54*.

their self-revelations and the Doctor's final action. At this stage, however, his demand enables the audience to hear more about the Doctor's treatment of her patients, that both Beutler and Ernesti are incurable and that both 'Unglücksfälle' were 'nicht vorauszusehen', but could have been committed by anyone, herself or the Inspector, for example. At this stage this seems to be a perfectly reasonable assumption — providing, of course, that both were sane (p.19/p.27).

It only remains for the Inspector to be told in significant detail about the two physicists, that they might well have been affected by the radioactive material with which they have been working, about the Doctor herself, that she comes from an old family and that it is almost a miracle 'wenn ich für relativ normal gelten darf' (p.21/p.29) — does the audience suspect anything here? — and that the third patient, Johann Wilhelm Möbius, has been here for fifteen years, has had nothing to do with radioactivity and is harmless.

When the Inspector departs, we realize that he has served the purpose of the classical exposition: the audience now knows what has gone before and the present situation of the plot now about to unfold. Before we leave the character, however, we must look further at his function in Act II; more will be said about the beginning of Act II when we examine it in more detail, but we note straightaway that the Inspector's role here is 'the same but different'; he has come to establish the facts but is now hardened to the conditions in Dr von Zahnd's asylum and will not be bullied any more. He smokes and drinks and shows appreciation of fine food and music. When he is finally granted his one long speech (p.57/pp.60-61), we realize that he is going to wash his hands of the whole affair and let the Doctor go her own way. He knows that he has found three murderers whom he cannot arrest, and need not, because he believes they are safely in the care of Dr von Zahnd and her three massive guards. At the end of the play, however, we realize the comic ambiguity of his assumption: the true reason was that the physicists were 'safe', because they were not insane. Thus the Inspector's cry: 'Die Gerechtigkeit macht zum ersten Male Ferien, ein immenses Gefühl', is also a delightfully ambiguous statement since it mocks one of Dürrenmatt's own often repeated credos: the belief that justice must be done, the basis of so many of his other works. When the Inspector adds: 'Die Gerechtigkeit, mein Freund, strengt nämlich mächtig an, man ruiniert sich in ihrem Dienst, gesundheitlich und moralisch, ich brauche einfach eine Pause', we recognize the voice of the world-weary Kommissär Bärlach in *Der Richter und sein Henker*, but only in his most pessimistic mood. Here the Inspector gives up, recognizes the hopelessness of trying to combat the power of the Doctor and her system. Bärlach and the other true Dürrenmattian characters would continue to fight.

The three nurses — Dorothea Moser, Irene Straub and Monika Stettler — along with the Senior Nurse, Marta Boll, are also rather more than mere walk-on parts. Indeed, they bring the plot into being, since there would have been no need for a plot had they not been strangled. To establish their identities, firstly Dorothea Moser ('mosern' means 'to complain'): she was Beutler's nurse whom, he declares, he loved, but whom he has strangled (on 12 August) with a curtain cord because, as we later learn, she suspected that he was not mad. As he says: 'es galt, meinen Wahnsinn durch einen Mord endgültig zu beweisen' (p.60/p.63). Although blonde and 'biegsam', her build, her 'Körperfülle', and the fact that she was a wrestler ('Mitglied des Damenringvereins', p.6/p.16), indicated that she was not quite the normal, gentle, caring nurse. While Dorothea is now just a memory, when the curtain rises we can see Irene Straub as a corpse, albeit in the background 'in tragischer und definitiver Stellung' (p.3/p.13), and in the 1980 version we read that the police '[ziehen] die Kontouren der Leiche mit Kreide nach usw' (p.14), so that something of her remains on stage when the body is removed. Irene, twenty-two, was Einstein's nurse whom he has just strangled, three months after Dorothea's murder, but with the flex of the standard lamp, instead of the curtain cord which Beutler had used.

Dürrenmatt's revised stage direction allows Einstein to go upstage later and muse reflectively on the corpse's contours. He tells us that her love was all-embracing and, although he treated her 'like a dog', she wanted to marry him and return to her little village of Kohlwang. He sums up her behaviour in one of Dürrenmatt's seemingly misogynous aphorisms: 'Es gibt nichts Unsinnigeres auf der Welt als die Raserei, mit der sich die Weiber aufopfern' (pp.43-44/p.48). Irene too was well built ('Landmeisterin des nationalen Judoverbandes'), which allows the audience at least a smile at the thought of these powerful young women being strangled by two supposedly old academics. Yet she too had become suspicious and had had to be silenced, 'um eure geheime Mission nicht zu gefährden,' as Möbius tells the scientists in Act II (p.75/p.75).

The Oberschwester, Marta Boll, is much the same type. She too is a physically strong woman: 'Ich stemme,' she tells the Inspector (p.6/p.16), and her confident, almost arrogant attitude to the Doctor shows that she knows her worth. She is, however, only part of the exposition with the Inspector and serves otherwise only to indicate that the patients must have been well cared for, since she is so sorry to leave them. That her and Schwester Monika's job has to be taken over by three muscular (male) 'Pfleger', might be thought to be a reflection on the mores of the 1960s.

The case and the role of Monika Stettler are however quite different: she is the nurse of one of the two main characters and, unlike Dorothea and Irene, is not a sportswoman but rather a sensitive, caring person: 'Monika Stettler war meine beste Pflegerin,' says Dr von Zahnd, 'Sie verstand die Kranken. Sie konnte sich einfühlen' (p.51/p.55). This very sympathetic understanding causes her death, because through this understanding nature she realized that Möbius was not mad. We first meet Monika after the Rose Family has departed, and we learn immediately that she has seen through Möbius' act with his wife Lina when he pretended to be insane and to have spoken to his King Solomon, and she adds: 'Sie handelten planmäßig', another clue for the audience that Möbius is not what he is pretending to be. It is a very significant sentence for the action when we consider Point 9 at the end of the text about 'planmäßig vorgehende Menschen'.

When Monika tells Möbius that she is to be moved into the main building to be replaced by the 'Pfleger', Möbius confesses how much she has meant to him during the past two years. However, he is still acting, for when Monika says that she does not believe that he is mad and that she too believes in the 'miracle' of King Solomon,

'Möbius starrt sie fassungslos an'. And she must believe him, because she knows that he is not insane: 'Ich weiß einfach, daß Sie nicht krank sind. Ich fühle es' (p.41/p.46). Möbius, Monika feels, is like herself, alone in the world; she has conscientiously served her patients for five years 'im Namen der Nächstenliebe', has sacrificed her life to them, and now she wants to sacrifice herself for one person only: 'Ich habe doch auch niemanden mehr auf der Welt als Sie!' she cries hysterically (p.45/p.50). Möbius is horrified and amazed to hear of the plans that she has already made for their life together: 'Ich will mit Ihnen schlafen, ich will Kinder von Ihnen haben' (p.45/p.49); she has taken on a new job in her home town of Blumenstein, she has saved up money for them, she has even contacted his former teacher, Professor Scherbert (is the name perhaps just too near to 'Scherbett'?) who will read Möbius' manuscript and assure his future. But most important of all, Monika feels, 'Fräulein Doktor von Zahnd hat schon alles geregelt. Sie hält Sie zwar für krank, aber für ungefährlich' (p.47/p.51),[16] a fine example of Monika's misunderstanding of the Doctor's motives and an illustration of that very Point 9 about 'planmäßig vorgehende Menschen'. The Doctor has indeed arranged everything, but not quite as Monika thinks.

The matter of King Solomon will be dealt with more fully when I come to discuss Möbius himself. Monika believes that he appears to Möbius, simply because he says that he does — and she loves Möbius. She is unaware, as we shall see, of what Möbius really means by 'König Salomo' and she betrays this when she says: 'Und wenn Sie erzählten, auch noch der König David erscheine Ihnen mit seinem Hofstaat, würde ich es glauben' — why? — 'Ich weiß einfach, daß Sie nicht krank sind' (p.41/p.46). She sees in Möbius a man rejected by the world and she simply wants to make

---

[16] One of the major changes in the 1980 version is that from p.45/p.50 on: Möbius and Monika address each other as 'du'; 'Liebst du mich denn gar nicht?' asks Monika 'verzweifelt'. In the Nelson edition, it occurs very suddenly within Monika's speech on p.48: 'Ich bin da, dir zu helfen', shortly before the murder. It could certainly be argued that the first version is more dramatic. The change was probably made because of the much wider use of 'du' since 1962.

him happy. When (in the 1980 version) she comes back into the darkened room with his manuscripts to prepare for the departure on the 8.20 train to Blumenstein, she is blissful with tears of happiness in her eyes, and she dies like this with the curtain cord that killed Dorothea Moser round her throat. Her death is the catalyst for the physicists' actions in the second act.

Two aspects of Swiss life are mocked with the appearance of the Rose Family: the bourgeois complacency and the religious fervour of some parts of Protestant Switzerland. Although one could certainly defend Frau Rose as some critics have tried to do (cf. Durzak in *30*, pp.121-22), as a hard-working divorcee, a mother who has had to bring up three sons on her own and has financed Möbius' fifteen-year stay in the sanatorium, she is nevertheless mocked by the author as a rather sentimental do-gooder who has now married one of her own type. She can be mocked mainly, of course, through her language, although a good director would no doubt dress her appropriately also. Her first words: 'Ich muß Sie ganz grausam überraschen, Fräulein Doktor' (p.23/p.31), to say that she has married a missionary, are a comic over-statement, especially as she 'errötet und weist etwas unbeholfen auf ihren neuen Mann'. (Since it is now November and they met in September, they can only have been married since October, that is, three weeks before). The Doctor's brusque response to her anguish is a typical Dürrenmattian *Kalauer*: 'Das Leben hat weiterzublühen', which might be expected of a future life with the 'Roses'.

Frau Rose describes her early life with Möbius. She obviously came from a well-off family whereas he was a working-class orphan, and it certainly underlines her merits that she helped him financially through his leaving certificate and university physics course until they married — clearly in the middle of his studies, since he was twenty and she twenty-five. (This information is omitted in the 1980 version, cf. p.26/p.33). While Möbius was writing his doctoral dissertation, she worked to keep the family going: four years after marriage along came Adolf-Friedrich (now sixteen), then Wilfried-Kaspar (now fifteen) and finally Jörg-Lukas who is said to be fourteen — but if so, Möbius' 'fifteen years' in the asylum must be a rough estimate. Just when a professorship was in sight, however, Möbius fell ill and she had to work in Tobler's chocolate factories — another 'Swiss' clue — to pay for his treatment.

Her reasons for remarrying are not made completely clear. She blames herself for leaving Möbius, but can only say that she did not remarry because keeping Möbius in the sanatorium was going beyond her means; indeed life, she says, is actually harder for her now, since her new husband already has six children. Thus we must assume that she remarried for love — and religion; her whole bearing and her language will demonstrate her wish to be a missionary's wife. Her conversation with her ex-husband betrays both her sentimentality and her uncertainty. To address Möbius, a university-trained scientist, by the pet diminutive 'Johann Wilhelmlein' had already been mocked by the Doctor, hard-bitten as she is (p.29/p.35), but Frau Rose continues to use it. Of course her visit marks the audience's first sight of Möbius, and it will assume that Möbius is indeed insane, particularly when he declaims his frightening 'Psalm Salomos'. Even his conversation with his three sons would only give a slight clue as to his true state of mind. The eldest boy wants to study theology and the second philosophy; only when the third mentions that he wants to become a physicist does Möbius react as a man driven insane by his profession might well do. He forbids his son to follow that profession; indeed we hear him claim that he would not be in an asylum at all had he not become a physicist, and that they all, including the family, know that he is there because he must be insane because his King Solomon appears to him.

Dürrenmatt tries to contrast the innocence of the three boys with Möbius' wild 'insanity' by having them play a piece by Buxtehude on their recorders. It seems to me to be one of the few unsuccessful scenes in the play — too sentimental and too improbable. Its one merit is that it underlines the sentimental religiosity of Oskar Rose, Frau Rose's missionary husband. He is portrayed as the standard meek and mild curate, always ready with a sickly biblical quotation to meet the minute: 'Der Herr ist mein Hirte, mir wird nichts mangeln' (Psalm 23. 1). It has not escaped our notice that Frau Rose has stressed that he is a 'leidenschaftlicher Vater' who has already brought six children into the world. There is therefore more than a slight suspicion of hypocrisy here in the good man's character; he is not all that other-worldly, and it makes Frau Rose's assertion that he is not very robust a cue for audience laughter.

His major function in the scene is to allow us to hear Möbius' outburst, for Frau Rose tells us: 'Oskar kennt alle Psalmen auswendig. Die Psalmen Davids, die Psalmen Salomos' (p.33/p.39). Relying on an audience's knowledge of the gentle and erotically beautiful nature of the *Song of Solomon*, Dürrenmatt is able to achieve a climactic effect by having Möbius contradict so violently the meek Oskar's protest that King Solomon would have enjoyed 'das Flötenspiel dieser unschuldigen Knaben' (p.34/p.40).[17]

The second group of minor characters would come into the category of what in German is known as 'Statisten' (i.e. walk-on characters), usually not of first importance for the plot, but essential nevertheless. In a Dürrenmatt *Komödie*, they usually take over the role of what were called *bomolochoi*, the buffoons, in the Old Greek comedy, whose prime function was to cause laughter. This is the function here of Sievers, McArthur and Murillo, and, to a lesser extent, the two policemen.[18]

Sievers, McArthur and Murillo are the three 'Pfleger', a term usually translated as 'male nurse', but here clearly a euphemism for 'guard' or 'Wärter'; yet the term is first used by Einstein when he says that Newton and he will have to shoot each other and the guards

---

[17] The Book of Psalms in the Old Testament (between The Book of Job and The Proverbs) contains 150 psalms, many of them specifically subtitled 'A Psalm of David' (who was Solomon's father). Proverbs is followed by Ecclesiastes and then come the eight chapters of The Song of Solomon, called 'Das Hohe Lied' in German. It has the most beautiful and erotic chapters of the Old Testament, cf. these relevant lines: 'Ich bin eine Blume zu Saron und eine Rose im Tal (2. 1), and 'Deine zwei Brüste sind wie zwei Rehzwillinge, die unter den Rosen weiden' (4. 5) (cf. p.34/p.40).

[18] The two policemen have really no dramatic function - although it might just be noted that, in Swiss German, 'ein Blocher' is a 'floor polisher', and that *Guhl* and *Güllen* bear a slight resemblance.

(p.70/p.71). Technically they only become 'Wärter' when they appear in their black uniforms and carrying pistols (p.78/p.78). Dürrenmatt obviously had the fairly traditional Central European's view of the USA in 1961, that is, a 'Kontinent der unbegrenzten Möglichkeiten', as it is often called, its free economy manipulated by gangsters and cliques. We saw how Claire's bodyguards in *Der Besuch der alten Dame* were murderers, released specially from the electric chair in Sing-Sing at her behest at a cost of a million dollars each. Now we have three 'riesenhafte' men, one (probably McArthur) a negro, who take the same role (eventually) in this play. (We are reminded too of Gastmann's two 'Diener' in *Der Richter und sein Henker*.) The two Pfleger have interesting names: McArthur reminds us of the US general, Douglas McArthur (1880-1964), who was Commander of the US Forces in the Far East at the time of the dropping of the atomic bombs on Japan; Murillo was the name of Bartolomé Esteban Murillo (1618-82), a Spanish painter, whose speciality was Heaven-aspiring madonnas whom he painted in wonderfully innocent blues and whites; Uwe Sievers, the Oberpfleger, has of course a German name which, along with the black uniforms, the gun and the harsh, staccato 'Rauskommen', ordering the physicists from their rooms in Act III for the confrontation with the Fräulein Doktor (p.80/p.79), would remind any public in 1962 of the unforgettable SS or Gestapo. (The suggestion that the Sievers name was meant, impishly, to resemble that of Germany's top soccer star, Uwe Seeler, is probably not to be taken seriously, although Dürrenmatt was very knowledgeable about football.)

When we first see these three men, however, we are made to smile by a neat Dürrenmattian paradox: these ox-like heavies serve the most refined food on the finest porcelain, Meißen, the blue and white porcelain still regarded as the finest in Europe; and they serve it with the choicest German(ic) manners: as they leave, 'die drei verbeugen sich' and Sievers says to the Inspector: 'Herr Inspektor, wir hatten die Ehre', a typical middle-class German expression, but hardly the language one would expect to hear from a former European heavyweight champion (Sievers), a South American heavyweight champion (Murillo) or a North American middleweight champion (McArthur). The gourmet meal, served on delicate porcelain by these incongruous monsters, allows that 'Frösteln' once again to creep down our spines.[19] This is a fine example of the grotesque, where reality is perverted. L.B. Jennings' view that the grotesque was the 'demonic made ludicrous' (*49*, p.690), and Wolfgang Kayser's assertion that it destroys 'grundsätzlich die Ordnungen und zieht den Boden fort' (*52*, p.384), seem particularly apposite there.

---

[19]Dürrenmatt was a well-known bon viveur whose extensive wine cellar was always generously opened for his guests. References to gourmet food appear in almost all of his works, e.g. the meal served up to Tschanz by Bärlach at the end of *Der Richter und sein Henker* and Traps's meal in *Die Panne*; but they are always, as here, 'Henkersmahlzeiten', that is, meals for the condemned man.

7. Die Physiker: *The Major Characters and the Dramatic Structure*

We turn now to the four major characters in the play, all of whose roles are entwined or 'verzahnt', one might say, a thought which has led many a commentator to suggest that it is the origin of the Fräulein Doktor's name, von Zahnd, but, as with Tschanz, it is a not uncommon Swiss name (cf. footnote 4 on p.31).

Since Dürrenmatt's view is that nuclear fission was, literally, a dangerous, deadly invention and scientists had been criminally responsible for letting it loose on the world, and had then been naively complacent enough to believe that they could somehow escape the consequences of their criminal act, we can appropriately begin this chapter with a study of the three scientists.

If we try to see Beutler and Ernesti through the eyes of a member of the audience or the reader of the play, experiencing the work for the first time, then we have, at first sight, a not unfamiliar comic asylum scene, the subject, alas, of many a bar-room joke, TV or film plot. In Switzerland itself, there are many such jokes which related to the 'Webstübeli' in the local asylum on the Zürichberg, the 'Burghölzli'. The incongruity of Beutler's first appearance 'in einem Kostüm des beginnenden achtzehnten Jahrhunderts mit Perücke' (p.8/p.18) and his opening words to the Inspector: 'Sir Isaac Newton', would make our spectator smile, as would the ensuing disjointed and illogical conversation, a type so often associated with the mentally deranged. Beutler's remark that he had become a physicist only 'aus Ordnungsliebe [...]. Um die scheinbare Unordnung in der Natur auf eine höhere Ordnung zurückzuführen' (p.9/p.19), would only be seen in retrospect as a 'clue'. At first sight too, Beutler's claim that he is not Newton, but is in reality Einstein, seems puzzling, for it plays no further part in the plot until von Zahnd denies the fact to the

Inspector. It does, however, allow the author to introduce the major issue — the invention of the atomic bomb — in the middle of this seemingly illogical conversation. The Inspector is embarrassed and confused by this weird figure in eighteenth-century dress, but we, the audience, while smiling at the incongruities, are actually being given the reasons for the three physicists' dilemma: is it more criminal to have invented the atomic bomb or to have murdered a nurse, asks Beutler (p.13/p.22). But the basic question is hidden for the moment under the verbiage about switching on the electric light: the audience hears the question, but is immediately distracted and amused when Beutler admits that he does not understand electricity either.

The critic Walter Kerr wrote once that the sign of the ampersand (&) always 'suggests comedy' and one thinks straightaway of Laurel and Hardy, Abbott and Costello, Morecambe and Wise; the author certainly does make 'Newton and Einstein' look and sound like a comic duo; the latter's first appearance in Einsteinian disguise — 'Hager, schlohweiße lange Haare, Schnurrbart' — carrying a violin (p.18/p.26) and fighting off sleep, does marry well with the Newtonian persona. Ernesti-Einstein has been in the sanatorium for two years, Beutler for one, which makes it strange that their respective governments took so long to set them on to Möbius, who had been there for fifteen years, that is, since the end of the war.

The comic in the characters — and they are meant to be comic — comes with their first illogical and incongruous statements. The introduction told us that they were 'harmlose, liebenswerte Irre, lenkbar, leicht zu behandeln und anspruchslos' (p.3/p.13), and both Beutler and Ernesti behave accordingly on their first appearance. As Möbius works himself up to strangling his Monika, Einstein appears at his door to say, in a gentle, absent-minded way: 'Ich erdrosselte Schwester Irene' (p.42/p.47) and wondered if he would ever play his violin again. When Möbius tells him that he had just been playing the Kreutzer Sonata while the police were present, Einstein answers inconsequentially: 'Die Kreutzersonate. Gott sei Dank' and adds: 'Dabei geige ich gar nicht gern und die Pfeife liebe ich auch nicht. Sie schmeckt scheußlich' — another clue for the audience, since

Einstein's pipe, like Hitler's little moustache and Churchill's cigar,
had belonged to his public persona since the war. So this Einstein is
an impostor. His final words to Monika before the murder,
'Gehorchen Sie Ihrem Geliebten und fliehen Sie!', show that he is
anything but what Monika calls him: 'Dieser arme irre Mensch.'
Thus the audience and the reader are confronted in Act I with two
harmless inmates about whom they know really very little. The
Doctor has suggested that they are both incurable (p.19/p.27) and
that the illness stems from their involvement with radioactivity
which might have altered their mental processes. She absolves
herself therefore from any involvement in their crimes, which makes
her statement in Act II — that she had driven the nurses to force
their attentions on the physicists — all the more dramatic.

Since, however, Act II presents us with two very different
personae, it might now be useful to consider the third physicist and
his relationship to them: one of the two main characters, Johann
Wilhelm Möbius. Arthur Taylor tentatively suggests (*13*, pp.97-98)
that the choice of name was 'probably a tribute' to August Ferdinand
Möbius (1790-1868) and his 'Möbius-Fläche' or 'Möbius-strip', still
played with by children in primary schools, the main property of
which was that when the two sides of the strip were turned and glued
together to form a ring and this was cut down the middle, one was
left, not with two rings, but paradoxically with one large ring. This
explanation for Dürrenmatt's choice of name has now been widely
accepted, as has the phonemic similarity between Möbius and
Oedipus since Dürrenmatt's spoof interview, *Friedrich Dürrenmatt
interviewt F.D.* of 1981 (WA25, pp.139-67). This is the writer's own
interpretation of the play, given there; it merits quotation:

> *Die Physiker* denken das Ödipus-Motiv weiter. An die
> Stelle des Orakels ist die Wissenschaft getreten. Der
> Wissenschaftler ist in der Lage, abschätzen zu können,
> was die Ergebnisse seiner Forschung unter Umständen
> zu bewirken vermögen: die Vernichtung der Menschheit.
> Möbius versucht, den Gefahren seiner physikalischen
> Ergebnisse dadurch zu entgehen, daß er sich ins

Irrenhaus flüchtet. Er stellt sich verrückt. Dieses entspricht der Flucht des Ödipus vor dem Schicksal, das ihm das Orakel ankündigt, nach Theben. Hier greift der Zufall ein. Ödipus flüchtet in die falsche Stadt, Möbius in das falsche Irrenhaus. Indem die verrückte Irrenärztin Mathilde von Zahnd die gespielte Verrücktheit des Möbius als Wahrheit auffaßt und somit seine Entdeckungen, die sie sich aneignet, nicht als Verrücktheit, sondern als das ansieht, was sie sind, als geniale Entdeckungen, hebt sie den Sinn seiner Flucht auf. Möbius and seine zwei Genossen, gleichfalls Physiker, verhalten sich wie drei Reisende, die, in den falschen Zug gestiegen, nach hinten rennen, um so doch noch den Ort zu erreichen, von dem sich der Zug in rasender Fahrt immer weiter entfernt.

(WA25, pp.150-52)

This useful digest of the play shows us how the author wished this major character to be presented. Further in the interview Dürrenmatt reminded us that the Doctor was originally intended to be male — we recall how the Claire character in *Der Besuch der alten Dame* was also originally male — but that the celebrated German actress, Therese Giehse, who did create the Claire character in the earlier play and was to have a great success in her role in Dürrenmatt's later play *Der Meteor* (1966), had read the first version and wanted to play the part. So Dürrenmatt made the Doctor a female. The change undoubtedly benefited the action, since there was now a sex clash as well as a personality clash between the two main characters. We already had the personality clash in the three physicists' characters: two power-seeking political figures versus one idealist, fighting for (his version of) the truth.

Dürrenmatt introduces his main male figure cleverly. Before his entrance, we have met everybody else of importance: the Doctor, the Inspector, Beutler and Ernesti, Marta Boll and the Rose Family, in other words all those who have a connection with Möbius. Significantly, the one remaining important figure, Schwester

Monika, appears when all the others have left him — their business is their own, between them alone. We have therefore a fairly full picture of Möbius before he appears, 'ein vierzigjähriger, etwas unbeholfener Mensch' (p.29/p.35), a description which could well have been of the author in 1961-62. Dürrenmatt has always been fond of casting his major characters in his own image.

What do we know of Möbius before his entrance? From Dr von Zahnd, we learned that he is different from the other two patients: although a physicist like them, he had not worked with radioactivity (she claimed) and had been in the asylum for fifteen years, much longer, therefore, than the other two. We heard too that his condition is harmless and unchanged (p.21/p.29). When Frau Rose, his former wife, appears, we learn further that Möbius was a working-class orphan whom she had helped through his studies and married when he was twenty. The new, important fact that we learn from the conversation is that Möbius continues to claim that he is visited regularly by King Solomon. After berating the missionary for failing to accept these visitations as genuine ('Als Theologe müssen Sie doch immerhin mit der Möglichkeit eines Wunders rechnen', p.25/p.33), the Doctor claims that her task as psychiatrist is not to decide whether these 'Erscheinungen' are genuine or not, but simply to care for the medical condition of her patients, a remark which will be seen in retrospect to be part of her 'disguise'.

Supplied with all of this information, we are now ready to meet Möbius, a rather distraught, absent-minded man who slowly remembers his three children, but who only, and significantly, comes alive when the third boy, Jörg-Lukas, admits that he wants to become a physicist. Is Möbius' reaction genuine, or is it faked? Does he want to justify his mask of insanity? I think that the remark is genuine, for in the next minute he relapses into his feigned insanity by claiming that they all take him to be mad just because King Solomon appears to him. Jörg-Lukas's remark reveals Möbius' true self and his feeling of guilt. Thus it is when the children play their Buxtehude piece on their recorders that Möbius can display his 'madness': when Oskar Rose protests that King Solomon, above all, would have enjoyed this innocent music-making and mentions

'Salomo, der Psalmendichter, Salomo, der Sänger des Hohen Liedes', Möbius can spit out his terrible 'Psalm Salomos, den Weltraumfahrern zu singen' (pp.34-35/pp.41-42). It will be recalled that the Soviets had just sent Yuri Gagarin into space in 1961 and that Robert Jungk's book *Heller als tausend Sonnen* was being widely discussed in German-speaking countries. It would also need an audience familiar with the Bible and with the gentle, but highly erotic *Song of Solomon* to appreciate truly Möbius' vicious parody of it, a prophetic indictment of the wasting of the earth and an indication of Dürrenmatt's interest in and knowledge of the solar system, displayed again in his later play on the theme *Porträt eines Planeten* (WA12, 1970). The 1980 version of the scene makes the psalm much more dramatic by distributing some of the interjections to Frau Rose ('Aber Johann Wilhelm'), Missionär Rose ('Herr Möbius'), the three boys ('Papi'), Frau Rose again ('Johann Wilhelmlein! Mein lieber Johann Wilhelmlein!'), then finally in this version, Marta Boll, who has entered silently with Monika to say 'Aber Herr Möbius'. All these interjections are now in the text of Möbius' outburst and make it much more dramatic. The entry of Schwester Monika that little bit earlier also ensures that she has heard at least part of his ranting and she is therefore more able to agree that Möbius had been a little too violent, and indeed that he had feigned the whole affair.

It has often been asserted that, if Möbius had really loved Monika, he could never have brought himself to strangle her, but as the author himself wrote in his 'interview', that is the point of the scene: 'nur wenn Möbius wirklich liebe, werde die Szene ungeheuerlich' (WA25, p.151). He had to murder her to prevent her from enticing him back into a world in which his discoveries would be fatal. He killed her because he loved her. The temptation had to be removed for the good of the world. The other two scientists, we learn later, killed at the behest of the governments who controlled them, although Dr von Zahnd will have a word to say about that view later (see p.109 below).

At the end of Act I Möbius is a sorry figure with tears in his eyes. Monika has told him that she believes that King Solomon appears to him, a chosen one: '[...], die Weisheit des Himmels wurde dir zuteil' (p.48/p.52), but she also believes that Solomon's message means that Möbius must leave the asylum and fight for his beliefs in the wide world outside. Since he dare not do this, he murders her. The act closes on an anticlimax, with Newton observing the latest corpse and Einstein playing Kreisler's *Schön Rosmarin*, a piece of sentimental Viennese music, and we recall Ophelia's words in Shakespeare's *Othello*: 'There's rosemary, that's for remembrance.'

Act I is therefore, as Dürrenmatt had promised in the introduction, a sort of 'satyr play', the comedy which followed the tragedy and reversed or travestied its theme. The structure of the play is clearly a parody of the classical tragedy's dramatic conventions; the Unities of Time, Place and Action seem certainly to be observed in this *Komödie*: the play will be acted in the time which passes on the stage; the scene never changes and there is only one plot. There are also few characters and a good deal of the language is in that classical 'stichomythic' (albeit unrhymed) mode. But Act II parodies Act I itself. The opening scene of Act II 'reverses' the opening of Act I: there the Inspector is allowed neither to smoke nor to drink, in Act II he is immediately offered a Havana cigar and a glass of schnaps; Voß calls the perpetrator of the second crime a 'Mörder' in Act I and is stiffly corrected by Marta Boll to the 'Täter'; in Act II the Doctor calls Ernesti 'den Mörder' and is immediately corrected, by Voß, to 'den Täter'. This is all neatly balanced by the almost word-for-word repetition of some of the dialogue, as for example:

> Inspektor: Haben Sie die Aussagen der Oberschwester, Guhl?
> Guhl: Jawohl, Herr Inspektor.
>   (Act I)

> Inspektor: Haben Sie die Aussagen, Guhl?
> Guhl: Jawohl, Herr Inspektor.
>   (Act II)

The Inspector's questioning of Marta Boll in Act I and of the Doctor in Act II (from 'Wie hieß die Schwester?' pp.5 and 50/pp.15 and 54) in stichomythic sentences is obviously meant for comic effect before the 'comedy' of Act I darkens into the 'tragedy' of Act II.

That Dürrenmatt should have taken specifically Sophocles' *Oedipus* as his model Greek tragedy is also interesting, for in many ways the Oedipus story is untypical of classical Greek tragedy. As Harsh rightly claims, 'the plot is unusual, for it does not concern any fatal error which occurs during the action of the play' — that *hamartia* of which I wrote earlier (see above, p.59). Harsh continues: 'The basic theme of the *Oedipus* is the irony of fate' (*39*, p.112), and it is this concept which Dürrenmatt parodies with his concept of chance or *Zufall*. 'Die Kunst des Dramatikers besteht darin, in einer Handlung den Zufall möglichst wirksam einzusetzen' (Point 5, p.89/p.91). He buttresses this concept by employing throughout the play what Western readers will naturally take as one of the generally accepted symbols of fortune, luck and chance: the number three. From the Christian concept of the Holy Trinity (Father, Son and Holy Ghost) on, the number three has played an important role in Western symbolism. It, and its fellows seven and twenty-one, have been regarded as symbols of good fortune. (We might take the menorah, the symbolic seven-branched candelabra of the ancient Jewish temple as an example too.)

The number three is employed throughout this play — we can assume deliberately — as a travesty of the familiar German proverb: 'Aller guten Dinge sind drei' ('all good things come in threes'), because in this play, and in Act II particularly, this is obviously not the case. Let us examine in more detail how Dürrenmatt makes use of this symbolism:

1. There are three scientists: Möbius, Kilton and Eisler.
2. Three nurses are murdered: Dorothea, Irene and Monika.
3. There are three Pfleger: Sievers, McArthur and Murillo.
4. Fräulein Doktor von Zahnd had three ancestors: August, Joachim and Leonidas von Zahnd.

5. Dorothea's death took place three months before the play begins.
6. Frau Rose was married three weeks before the meeting with Möbius.
7. The three rooms on the stage are numbered 1, 2 and 3 throughout the action, and three chairs remain there too.
8. Möbius' colleagues each parade three names: Beutler-Newton-Kilton and Ernesti-Einstein-Eisler.
9. Möbius has three children each with (it could be claimed) three names: Adolf-Friedrich Möbius, Wilfried-Kaspar Möbius and Jörg-Lukas Möbius.
10. Möbius repeats his final dramatic statement, the last word of the play, three times: 'Ich bin Salomo, ich bin Salomo, ich bin der arme König Salomo'.
11. The twenty-one of the twenty-one Punkte is three times seven.

Is all this too far-fetched? I think not. The author is employing this numerological symbolism to parody that sense of deterministic fate (*moira*) which overhung the classical Greek tragedy and which was often travestied in the Greek satyr plays. We are dealing here with that 'indeterminacy' factor of Werner Heisenberg (see above, p.70) or, as Dürrenmatt put it brilliantly in Point 7, chance in a plot is conditioned by 'wann und wo wer zufällig wem begegnet' (p.89/p.91), and there must be few adults in the world who would not say 'amen' to that.

That Beutler and Ernesti meet Möbius in the asylum could not be considered a matter of pure chance, of course, as we hear when the confrontation scenes begin and Newton tells Möbius: 'Ein Geständnis, Möbius: Ich bin nicht verrückt' (p.59/p.62), and reveals to a shocked Möbius his true name: Alec Jasper Kilton, the formulator of the *Principle of Correspondence* (actually attributed to the Danish physicist and collaborator of Albert Einstein, Niels Bohr, 1885-1962). He has been sent by his government (clearly the USA) to spy on and eventually to abduct Möbius. Kilton is careful to mention that he only read Möbius' dissertation on his discoveries 'zufällig' (p.61/p.64), but his Secret Service decided that it wanted 'den genialsten Physiker der Gegenwart'. When 'Einstein' enters unobserved, the unmasking is completed; he is actually Joseph Eisler, the discoverer of the 'Eisler-Effekt' (who was in reality the Austrian Christian Johann Doppler, 1803-1853, the originator of the *Doppler Principle*). Eisler too is a Secret Service agent and, just as clearly, sent by the Soviets. In these scenes, Dürrenmatt manages to create that 'Frösteln' of which I have spoken by having the two 'spies' repeat each other's words in marionette-like phrases and which Henri Bergson, the French philosopher, in his seminal work *Le Rire* (1899) formulated as the essence of 'the comic': it is 'du mécanique plaqué sur du vivant' (*18*, p.29). The speakers act like inhuman 'things', puppets directed by an outside agency, or cartoon characters. Newton says: 'Meine Mission stand in Frage, das geheimste Unternehmen unseres Geheimdienstes' (p.60/p.63). Einstein repeats the phrase verbatim (p.63/pp.65-66); Newton and Möbius say to one another:

> Möbius: Verstehe.
> Newton: Befehl ist Befehl.
> Möbius: Selbstverständlich.
> Newton: Ich durfte nicht anders handeln.
> Möbius: Natürlich nicht.

> (p.60/p.63)

while Möbius and Einstein repeat this almost to the letter, except that Einstein's apology is rephrased, Luther-like: 'Ich konnte nicht anders handeln' (p.63/p.65). (It seems quite appropriate that the 'Western' agent should use 'durfte' and the 'Eastern' agent 'konnte'.)

Likewise, the comical mechanical ploy with the revolvers: this precedes both the 'Henkersmahlzeit' and the guards' brutal intervention and acts as a comic prelude to the (apparent) dénouement, the end of the conventional crime story when all is revealed (usually in the library). Möbius now admits why he sought asylum, in both senses of the word. Having thought up 'die einheitliche Feldtheorie', the unified theory of relativity, he had realized the awful consequences of his research: 'Neue, unvorstellbare Energien würden freigesetzt und eine Technik ermöglicht, die jeder Phantasie spottet, falls meine Untersuchung in die Hände der Menschen fiele' (pp.67-68/p.69). There then follows the first of three (!) speeches in which Möbius puts forward his argument for what he considers to be the responsibility of scientists vis-à-vis their world. In the first speech, he maintains that, as physicists, they must proceed in a scientific manner conditioned by logical conclusions. He points out that, although all three of them have the same goal, namely, to further the progress of science, their tactics are different: Kilton, for the Western powers, seeks to preserve the scientist's freedom of action and would therefore absolve the scientist from all responsibility ('Ob die Menschheit den Weg zu gehen versteht, den wir ihr bahnen, ist ihre Sache, nicht die unsrige', p.68/p.70). Eisler, for the Eastern powers, believes that, on the other hand, science should be subordinated to the power politics of the rulers ('Mir ist bloß mein Generalstab heilig. Wir liefern der Menschheit gewaltige Machtmittel. Das gibt uns das Recht, Bedingungen zu stellen', p.69/p.70).[20]

Möbius, asserting that his only freedom lies in the asylum, then tells his colleagues in his second speech how he gave up his family and his career because of these possible consequences of his research: 'Ich wählte die Narrenkappe,' he says and he pretended that King Solomon appeared to him, the only way out for men who have exceeded mankind's grasp: 'Unsere Wissenschaft ist schrecklich geworden, unsere Forschung gefährlich, unsere Erkenntnis tödlich,' and therefore: 'Wir müssen unser Wissen zurücknehmen, und ich habe es zurückgenommen' (p.74/p.74). And this is why Kilton and Eisler must stay in the asylum and tell their bosses that Möbius is

---

[20]Although space does not permit a fuller discussion, it should be noted that some elements of these speeches are either omitted or re-cast in the 1980 version. The overall effect is to bind Newton more firmly to the Western viewpoint and the freedom of the scientist, and Einstein to the Eastern view: the scientist's duty to the State — but both still accept that they are in Möbius' hands.

really insane, for only there, in the asylum, is there a chance of real freedom for all three.

Then, in his third and last speech, Möbius reminds them that they are all murderers: Kilton and Eisler killed their nurses for different reasons, it is true, says Möbius, but he killed Monika to prevent a greater killing: the deaths of thousands, what Bertolt Brecht once called 'das große Sterben'. So, must these murders remain senseless? 'Entweder haben wir geopfert oder gemordet,' says Möbius, 'Entweder bleiben wir im Irrenhaus, oder die Welt wird eines. Entweder löschen wir uns im Gedächtnis der Menschen aus, oder die Menschheit erlischt' (pp.75-76/pp.75-76). The tripartite nature of Möbius' speeches strike home like hammer blows. The men stand and drink, in marionette-like, serio-comic fashion, to their three dead nurses whom they sacrificed and for whom they will now follow the rational course of remaining in the asylum to preserve the secrets of their researches. The play seems to be reaching its conclusion: these highly intelligent physicists, students of the most rational of sciences, have seen the 'error of their ways' and, although they know that what they have invented could cause the end of the world, they will now let Möbius 'take back' his knowledge and bury it, with themselves, forever, deep in a Swiss sanatorium.

But the play is not at an end. Point 3 reads: 'Eine Geschichte ist dann zu Ende gedacht, wenn sie ihre schlimmstmögliche Wendung genommen hat.'

We last saw Fräulein Doktor von Zahnd when she took leave of the Inspector and his colleagues, a long time ago in the time span of the play, and it is indeed possible that some of the audience (or readers) have almost forgotten her. And what picture did they have of her when she left? We are told that she is about fifty-five with a hump on her shoulder, always dressed in her short doctor's white coat and with her stethoscope round her neck. She obviously came from a privileged family, her father, Geheimrat August von Zahnd having owned the villa which is now the sanatorium. An only child, she was hated by her father, a confirmed misogynist, who had seen what human catastrophes economic disasters could produce. When she claims that these were worse than anything that a psychiatrist sees, it is difficult to disagree, although we might just wonder what effect such a childhood must have had on her.

When we learn that her grandfather, Leonidas von Zahnd, was a field marshal responsible for losing a war in which many men had been slaughtered, we might appreciate her assertion that healthy people can murder as well — 'und bedeutend öfter' — than the insane. Thus, her claim that it is impracticable to lock up sick people like criminals seems to be only common sense and humane practice. Yet there have been two murders which make us at least query the success of her policy. Again, however, when the Inspector tells her that Newton thinks that he is Einstein and she replies that he is, in fact, Newton, because: 'Für wen sich meine Patienten halten, bestimme ich. Ich kenne sie weitaus besser, als sie sich selber kennen' (p.17/p.25), we sense a measure of force at odds with her otherwise enlightened pronouncements and actions, as when she accompanies Einstein as he plays his Beethoven.

When she reveals to the Inspector that Newton and Einstein were both atomic physicists and that it was just possible that their crimes were caused by an alteration to the brain due to the effects of radioactivity, for otherwise: 'Diese Unglücksfälle waren nicht vorauszusehen' (p.19/p.27), the audience might accept this as a possible explanation for two puzzling murders. The world had already been made aware in the recent past of the dangers of radioactivity and atomic science in a very spectacular way after all. Yet the first doubts about the Doctor should arise when she admits to the Inspector that it is indeed rather strange — she calls it, significantly, 'Schicksal' — that the money for her sanatorium had come from rich patients and from her relations because they had died (usually in her sanatorium) leaving her as the sole heiress. (And we hear that there are still two relations there, Tante Senta and Vetter Ulrich.) We know too from her title that she has never married — in our egalitarian age, she would be *Frau* Doktor, of course. Thus all the money was hers alone. But the most significant remark perhaps is yet to come: musing on the fact that she was always the sole heiress (and therefore reminding us that all her relations had died insane), she says that it is almost a medical miracle 'wenn ich für relativ normal gelten darf [...], was meinen Geisteszustand betrifft' (p.21/p.29).[21] There is at this stage no reason for doubting the truth of her statement; we shall recall it at the end of Act II.

It might just be worthwhile here to note how important the acting of the actress playing this role would be: she must not give any indication of anything abnormal in the character of the Doctor, the hump would be taken simply as a physical deformity, although those who had seen Dürrenmatt's *Der Besuch der alten Dame* might have suspicions. Her statements too would be taken at face value.

The Doctor becomes even more 'natural' and believable when the Rose family arrives and she treats them and their rather sentimental gentility with gentle, but determined mocking: 'Das Leben hat weiterzublühen,' she tells Frau Rose; she calls Möbius maternally 'unser guter Möbius', and defends his claim to have seen König Salomo, calling it a theological miracle. All in all, when she leaves the Möbius family together, having reassured them that there are plenty of financial resources available to maintain Möbius in the sanatorium, the audience has little or no reason to doubt that she is other than the distinguished (she has an honorary degree after all) head of a psychiatric unit.

Thus the end of Act I leaves us with a sense of bewilderment, even mystery. The dialogue, at first sight so rational, seems not quite that either of doctors or police inspectors; the characters likewise: the Doctor has the trappings of a rational scientist, yet, as we have seen, some of her remarks were strange, to say the least. The Inspector too seems to be the traditional sleuth of a crime story murder, and yet, after his conversations with Newton and the Doctor, he too takes on an aura of mystery. So, the climactic close of the act leaves the audience with many questions.

The word play between the Doctor and the Inspector at the beginning of Act II repeats the comic parodistic classic beginning to Act I, but now we find the Doctor seemingly truly upset at the loss of her 'favourite' nurse, Monika Stettler, even though what really worries

---

[21] The Routledge edition has 'relativ für normal'.

her is that her medical reputation will have been lost (p.52/p.56). Her attack on the murderer, Möbius, 'Sie haben meine beste Krankenschwester getötet, meine sanfteste Krankenschwester, meine süßeste Krankenschwester!' (p.54/p.58), with its serio-comic, tripartite form, is the last important remark that she makes before departing the scene, but it clearly changes the mood of the play. Möbius' chagrin as Monika's body is carried out leads shortly into the unveiling of the identities of his colleagues and takes us to what we have termed the first conclusion where the three physicists pledge themselves to remain in the asylum:

> Newton: Verrückt, aber weise.
> Einstein: Gefangen, aber frei.
> Möbius: Physiker, aber unschuldig.
>   (p.77/p.77)

The second conclusion is Dürrenmatt's dénouement and the illustration of Point 8: 'Je planmäßiger die Menschen vorgehen, desto wirksamer vermag sie der Zufall zu treffen' (p.90/p.91). Having congratulated themselves on having had the wisdom to choose an asylum as their hiding place and then having taken the seemingly rational decision to bury the results of their scholarly researches in this safe hiding place, the physicists are confronted with *Zufall*: of all the asylums in Switzerland, the one that they have chosen is run by a doctor who is not only insane herself, but who has the scientific nous to found a trust which, based on Möbius' discoveries, will 'die Länder, die Kontinente erobern, das Sonnensystem ausbeuten, nach dem Andromedanebel fahren' (p.85/p.85).

We know the truth when the Doctor tells the physicists: 'Auch mir ist der goldene König Salomo erschienen' (p.81/p.81), for Möbius has already told Monika that he has only pretended to see him (see above, p.99). Now the Doctor begins to speak in the heightened tones of the insane as she describes Solomon's appearance: 'Wie ein gewaltiger Engel', so that Einstein rightly says: 'Sie ist wahnsinnig geworden' (p.82/p.82). Yet the Doctor's insane monologues contain the truth of the play: scientists like Möbius cannot take back what they have discovered — theirs is the responsibility and theirs is the agony. What he discovered would in any case have been discovered by someone else: 'Alles Denkbare wird einmal gedacht. Jetzt oder in der Zukunft' (p.82/p.82), but the Doctor has discovered it now by copying Möbius' manuscripts before he destroyed them, and by driving her three nurses to make love to the men and, subsequently and consequently, to their deaths, she has made the three physicists murderers. Rather than destroying the evidence as they thought that they had done by murdering the nurses who had discovered their secret, they had been manipulated by the Doctor like puppets: 'Ihr wart bestimmbar wie Automaten und habt getötet wie Henker' (p.84/p.84). Now the asylum will become their prison in which they will serve their long sentences while the Doctor, like Dr Strangelove in Kubrick's film, will rule the world. Möbius' last words, which have been widely quoted — famously by President Jimmy Carter in a UN nuclear disarmament speech in 1977 — sum up the play: 'Was einmal gedacht wurde, kann nicht mehr zurückgenommen werden' (p.86/p.85). The action has taken 'the worst possible turn', and the three scientists can only recite their sad little lays before retiring, defeated, to what have now become their cells. While Newton and Einstein restrict themselves to an historical account of their lives and careers — Newton admitting that he had not fully solved the problem of gravity, and Einstein admitting, that although he loved mankind, he had recommended the construction of the atom bomb — Möbius now accepts the mask of his previously assumed madness and becomes King Solomon, once 'unermeßlich reich, weise und gottesfürchtig' but now no longer God-fearing, and the destroyer of his own empire by the misuse of his wisdom. The towns are now dead, his empire laid to waste and 'um einen kleinen, gelben, namenlosen Stern kreist, sinnlos, immerzu, die radioaktive Erde' (p.87/pp.86-87).

Like *Der Besuch der alten Dame*, *Die Physiker* has established itself as a classic of West European theatre and is performed regularly in many languages throughout the world. (In its greatest season,

1962-63, 1,598 performances in 59 theatres were listed.) Its theme had, of course, a certain immediacy; the two great ideologies were locked in verbal conflict, the threat of The Bomb hung over the whole world. When one watches or reads the play now, the theme has lost none of its relevance. Möbius' central statements: 'Wir müssen unser Wissen zurücknehmen, und ich habe es zurückgenommen' (p.74/p.74), and 'Entweder bleiben wir im Irrenhaus, oder die Welt wird eines' (pp.75/p.76) can be, and have been, applied to many of the ensuing political crises in the world. Hans Mayer perceptively linked Dürrenmatt's first statement with Adrian Leverkühn's remark in Thomas Mann's novel *Doktor Faustus* that the evil deeds perpetrated in the twentieth century — and particularly in Germany — should lead to the 'Zurücknahme' of the ideals of classical humanism, citing Beethoven's Ninth Symphony as the artistic work which would have to be sacrificed. Mayer sees Möbius' statement as the 'Zurücknahme des überlieferten Wissenschaftsideals', Leverkühn's as the 'Zurücknahme der bürgerlichen Ästhetik' (62, pp.98-99). Möbius has recognized the dangers of the success of his research and plans to nullify these by remaining in his asylum to prevent the world from becoming a madhouse. Yet it was Möbius' first decision to 'take back his knowledge' (that is, to recant, as Galilei did) by fleeing into an asylum, which led paradoxically to his surrendering that knowledge to a mad asylum director, Dr von Zahnd. Chance once again limited the scientist's rational thinking and proved to be that 'gap in his logic' of which Tiusanen wrote (see above, pp.17-18). Order and disorder, sanity and insanity, are pitted one against the other, the classical dramatic structure of the play against the irrational lunatic jokes, the seeming inevitablility of classical tragedy against the irrational workings of chance in what Dürrenmatt calls the 'unberechenbare Welt'.

It might well seem then that Dürrenmatt's play does present an 'Endsituation', and that he could be seen as the Bible-black pessimist whose 'final verdict, that the individual is impotent [...] is tantamount to the acknowledgement of a hopeless situation' (Knapp in 56, p.66). Such a view of the play has been taken by some of Dürrenmatt's later commentators like Knapp, influenced perhaps by the later plays such as *Porträt eines Planeten* (WA12, 1970), *Die Frist* (WA15, 1977) or *Achterloo* (*1*, 1983) which might also be taken as similar portents of doom and disaster. But such critics forget two important facts: firstly, that Dürrenmatt has always claimed that his works should be taken as warnings, not as prophecies. As far back as 1952, in an essay *Fingerübungen zur Gegenwart*, he wrote: 'Ich bin da, um zu warnen', and went on to compare himself as an author with the pilot guiding a ship into port: 'Noch *ist* das offene Meer, aber einmal werden die Klippen kommen, dann werden die Lotsen zu brauchen sein' (WA26, pp.31-32). *Die Physiker* (and many other Dürrenmatt plays) are warnings of what might happen if mankind continues to act irresponsibly and selfishly: 'Jeder Versuch eines Einzelnen, für sich zu lösen, was alle angeht, muß scheitern' (Point 18).

L.P. Johnson rightly asserts that 'this does not automatically mean pessimism', but adds perceptively, 'though you have to be courageous to remain cheerful in it', that is, in a world 'not foreseeably improvable' (*50*, p.138); which leads to the second point: it is often likewise overlooked that Dürrenmatt's works are meant to be played as *Komödien*, that is, they must be acted to bring about that mixture of 'satirischen Zorns' and the 'Bitterkeit der Ohnmacht' mentioned by Otto Rommel (see above, pp.15-16). 'Nichts schadet dieser Komödie, die tragisch endet, mehr als tierischer Ernst,' wrote Dürrenmatt in the *Anmerkung* at the end of *Der Besuch der alten Dame* (WA5, p.144), and that could apply to all of his *Komödien*. We could therefore draw this study to a conclusion with the closing words of the long *Nachwort zum Nachwort* of *Der Mitmacher: Ein Komplex*: 'Na schön, aber wie soll man das Ganze denn spielen? Und ich antworte, während mich die Nacht verschluckt [...]: Mit Humor' (WA14, p.328).

Select Bibliography

Friedrich Dürrenmatt's published works up to 1980 were collected in the *Werkausgabe* edited by Thomas Bodmer and published by Diogenes Verlag AG in Zürich in 1980. It contained twenty-nine volumes, with a thirtieth of critical writings, *Über Friedrich Dürrenmatt*. The works published therein and referred to in this book are denoted by WA. The works by Dürrenmatt in the first part of Section A below have all been published by Diogenes Verlag, Zürich since 1980.

A. OTHER PRIMARY TEXTS

1. *Achterloo* (1983) and *Achterloo IV* (1988).
2. *Justiz* (1985).
3. *Rollenspiele*, with Charlotte Kerr (1986).
4. *Der Auftrag* (1986).
5. *Versuche* (1988).
6. *Durcheinandertal* (1989).
7. *Turmbau,* containing *Stoffe iv-ix* (1990).
8. *Labyrinth,* containing *Stoffe i (Der Winterkrieg in Tibet)* and *Stoffe ii-iii (Mondfinsternis* and *Der Rebell,* both published originally in 1981-84) (1990).
9. *Kants Hoffnung* (1991).
10. *Midas oder Die schwarze Leinwand* (1991).
11. *Gedankenfuge* (1992).

Other works are being published posthumously.

Annotated editions

12. *Der Besuch der alten Dame,* ed. Paul Kurt Ackermann (London, Methuen, 1957; reprinted London, Routledge, 1990).
13. *Die Physiker,* ed. Arthur Taylor (London, Macmillan, 1966; reprinted Walton-on-Thames, Nelson, 1992).

Translations

14. *The Visit,* tr. Patrick Bowles (London, Cape, 1962).
15. *The Visit,* tr. Maurice Valency (New York, Samuel French, 1958).
16. *Four Plays: Romulus the Great, The Marriage of Mr Mississippi, An Angel Comes to Babylon* and *The Physicists,* (London, Cape, 1964).

B. SECONDARY LITERATURE

17. Arnold, A., *Friedrich Dürrenmatt* (Berlin, Colloquium, 1969).
18. Bergson, H., *Le Rire* (Paris, Presses Universitaires de France, 1901).
19. Bienek, H., 'Werkstattgespräch mit Friedrich Dürrenmatt', in *Neue Zürcher Zeitung,* 11 March 1962.
20. Boyd, U.D., *Die Funktion des Grotesken als Symbol der Gnade in Dürrenmatts dramatischem Werk* (Ph.D. dissertation, University of Maryland, 1964).
21. Brock-Sulzer, E., *Friedrich Dürrenmatt: Stationen seines Werkes* (Zürich, Arche, 1960).
22. ———, 'Friedrich Dürrenmatt: *Es steht geschrieben*', in *Die Tat,* 24 April 1947.
23. Buri, F., 'Der "Einfall" der Gnade in Dürrenmatts dramatischem Werk', in *36,* pp.35-69.
24. Butler, M., 'Das Labyrinth und die Rebellion', *Modern Languages,* 66/2 (1985), 104-08.
25. Butler, M., and M. Pender (eds), *Rejection and Emancipation: Writing in German-Speaking Switzerland, 1945-91* (Oxford, Berg, 1991). See introduction.
26. Dick, E.S., '*Der Besuch der alten Dame:* Welttheater und Ritualspiel', *Zeitschrift für deutsche Philologie,* 87 (1968), 498-509.
27. Diller, E., 'Aesthetics and the grotesque: Friedrich Dürrenmatt', *Drama Survey,* V (1966), 131-36.
28. ———, 'Friedrich Dürrenmatt's chaos and Calvinism', *Monatshefte,* Band 63, Heft 1 (1977), 28-40.
29. Donald, S.G., *Dürrenmatt:* Der Besuch der alten Dame (Glasgow, University of Glasgow French and German Publications, 1990).
30. Durzak, M., *Dürrenmatt, Frisch, Weiss* (Stuttgart, Reclam, 1972).
31. Esslin, M., 'Dürrenmatt — merciless observer', *Plays and Players,* 1963, 15-16.
32. ———, *The Theatre of the Absurd* (London, Eyre and Spottiswoode, 1962).
33. Fickert, K., 'Dürrenmatt's *The Visit* and *Job*', *Books Abroad, 41 (1968),* 389-92.
34. Goertz, H., *Dürrenmatt* (Rowohlt, Reinbek bei Hamburg, 1987).

35. Grimm, R., 'Parodie und Groteske im Werk Dürrenmatts', in *36*, pp.71-96.

36. Grimm, R., et al., *Der unbequeme Dürrenmatt* (Basel, Basilius, 1962).

37. Guthke, K.S., *Geschichte und Poetik der deutschen Tragikomödie* (Göttingen, Vandenhoeck und Ruprecht, 1961).

38. ——, *Modern Tragicomedy* (New York, Random House, 1966).

39. Harsh, P.W., *A Handbook of Classical Drama* (Stanford, Stanford University Press, 1944).

40. Hebbel, F., *Sämtliche Werke, historisch-kritische Ausgabe*, ed. R.M. Werner, 2nd ed. (Berlin, Behr, 1904).

41. Heidsieck, A., *Das Groteske und das Absurde im modernen Drama* (Stuttgart, Kohlhammer, 1969).

42. Helbling, R., 'Dürrenmatt criticism: exit the grotesque', in M. Lazar, *Play Dürrenmatt* (Malibu, Undena, 1983), pp.175-88.

43. ——, 'The function of the grotesque in Dürrenmatt', *Satire Newsletter*, No. IV (1966), 11-19.

44. ——, 'Groteskes und Absurdes — Paradox und Ideologie: Versuch einer Bilanz', in G. Knapp, *Friedrich Dürrenmatt* (Heidelberg, Lothar Stiehm, 1976), pp.233-53.

45. Holzapfel, R., 'The divine plan behind the plays of Friedrich Dürrenmatt', *Modern Drama*, VIII (1965), 237-46.

46. Hortenbach, J.C., 'Biblical Echoes in *Der Besuch der alten Dame*', *Monatshefte*, 57/4 (1965), 145-61.

47. Jauslin, C.M., *Friedrich Dürrenmatt: Zur Struktur seiner Dramen* (Zürich, Juris, 1964).

48. Jennings, L.B., 'Klein Zaches and his kin — the grotesque revisited', *Deutsche Vierteljahresschrift*, 44, Heft 4 (1970), 687-703.

49. ——, *The Ludicrous Demonic* (Berkeley, University of California Press, 1963).

50. Johnson, L.P., '"Verdauung" versus "Verfremdung": Dürrenmatt's position', in *Erbe und Umbruch in der neueren deutschsprachigen Komödie: Londoner Symposium 1987* (Stuttgart, Akademischer Verlag, 1990), pp.121-39.

51. Jünger, F.G., *Über das Komische* (Berlin, Klostermann, 1898).

52. Kayser, W., *Das Groteske* (Oldenburg, Stalling, 1957).

53. ——, *Das sprachliche Kunstwerk* (Francke, Bern, 1948).

54. Keel, D., *Friedrich Dürrenmatt: Denkanstöße* (Zürich, Diogenes, 1986).

55. Kerr, C. (director), *Porträt eines Planeten: Von und mit Friedrich Dürrenmatt* (film), in Süddeutscher Rundfunk III, 1984.

56. Knapp, G., 'Dürrenmatt's *Physicists* as a turning-point for the dramatist and his concept of history', in M. Lazar, *Play Dürrenmatt*, (Malibu, Undena, 1983), pp.55-66.

57. ———, '*Die Physiker*', in A. Arnold, *Interpretationen zu Friedrich Dürrenmatt* (Stuttgart, Klett, 1982), pp.97-109.
58. Knapp, G. und M., 'Recht — Gerechtigkeit — Politik', in H.G. Arnold (ed.), *Friedrich Dürrenmatt II* (München, text + kritik, 1976), pp.23-40.
59. Knapp, M., 'Die Verjüngung der alten Dame', in H.G. Arnold (ed.), *Friedrich Dürrenmatt II* (München, text + kritik, 1976), pp.58-66.
60. Knopf, J., *Der Dramatiker Friedrich Dürrenmatt* (Berlin, Henschel, 1987).
61. Kreuzer, F., *Die Welt als Labyrinth: Ein Gespräch mit Franz Kreuzer* (Zürich, Diogenes, 1986).
62. Mayer, H., 'Dürrenmatt und Brecht oder Die Zurücknahme', in *36* pp.97-116.
63. Morley, M., 'Dürrenmatt's dialogue with Brecht: a thematic analysis of *Die Physiker*', *Modern Drama*, 14 (1971-72), 232-42.
64. Murdoch, B., 'Dürrenmatt's *Physicists* and the tragic tradition', *Modern Drama*, 13 (1970), 270-75.
65. Peppard, M., *Friedrich Dürrenmatt* (New York, Twayne, 1969).
66. Preuss, J.W., 'Friedrich Dürrenmatt: Wie ein Drama entsteht', in C. Schmid und G. Simmerding (eds), *Literarische Werkstatt: Interviews mit Dürrenmatt, Zadek, Dorst, Handke, Nossack, Heißenbüttel, Grass, Wohmann, Bichsel und Johnson* (München, Oldenbourg, 1972), pp.9-18.
67. Reed, E.C., 'Friedrich Dürrenmatt's *Der Besuch der alten Dame*: a study in the grotesque', *Monatshefte*, LIII, Heft 1 (1961), 9-14.
68. Rock, D., 'A wager lost: some thoughts on the role of chance in Dürrenmatt', *Modern Languages*, 68/1 (1987), 22-27.
69. Roe, I., 'Dürrenmatt's *Die Physiker*/Die drei Leben des Galilei?', *Forum for Modern Language Studies*, XXVII/3 (1991), 255-67.
70. Rommel, O., 'Komik- und Lustspieltheorie', *Deutsche Vierteljahresschrift*, XXI/11 (1943), 252-86.
71. Rüedi, P., 'Friedrich Dürrenmatt', 13-part series in *Die Weltwoche*, 20.12.90-21.3.91.
72. Rülicke-Weiler, K., 'Leben des Galilei: Bemerkungen zur Schlußszene', *Sinn und Form*, 2 (1957), 232-312.
73. Sauter, R., 'Gespräch mit Dürrenmatt', *Sinn und Form*, 18/4 (1966), 1218-32.
74. Sophocles, *The Theban Plays*, tr. E. Watling (London, Penguin, 1947).
75. Steiner, G., *The Death of Tragedy* (London, Faber, 1961).
76. Tiusanen, T., *Dürrenmatt: A Study in Plays, Prose, Theory* (Princeton, Princeton University Press, 1977).
77. Whitton, K.S., 'Afternoon conversation with an uncomfortable person: interview with Dürrenmatt', *New German Studies*, 2/1 (1974), 14-30.

78. Whitton, K.S., *Dürrenmatt: Reinterpretation in Retrospect* (Oxford, Berg, 1990).
79. ———, 'Friedrich Dürrenmatt and the legacy of Bertolt Brecht', *Forum for Modern Language Studies*, XII/1 (1976), 65-81.
80. ———, *The Theatre of Friedrich Dürrenmatt* (London, Wolff, 1980).
81. Wright, A.M., 'Scientific method and rationality in Dürrenmatt', *German Life and Letters*, 35/1 (1981), 64-72.